They Walked With Jesus

Dolores Cannon

OZARK
MOUNTAIN
PUBLISHING

Originally published by Gateway Books,
The Hollies, Wellow, Bath, BA2 8QJ, United Kingdom.
First Printing 1994 | Reprinted: 1995
First American Printing: 2001 | Reprinted: 2010, 2011, 2012, 2013, 2015, 2016, 2018x2, 2019x2, 2020, 2023

Library of Congress Cataloging-in-Publication Data

Cannon, Dolores, 1931-2014
They Walked with Jesus by Dolores Cannon

Sequel to: Jesus and the Essenes. More eyewitness accounts of the missing portions of Jesus' life. The information was gained through regressive hypnosis, conducted by Dolores Cannon. Includes Bibliography.

1. Jesus. 2. History: Holy Land 3. Hypnosis 4. Reincarnation
I. Cannon, Dolores, 1931-2014 II. Title

Library of Congress Catalog Card Number: 99-076755
ISBN: 1-886940-09-6

Cover Design: Broadaway Printing
Book Design: Tom Cannon
Text set in Times New Roman

PO Box 754
Huntsville, AR 72740
www.ozarkmt.com

Contents

List of Illustrations

Chapter One

Discovering the Jesus Encounters

My work as a hypnotherapist specializing in reincarnation and past-life therapy has led me into strange situations and down mystifying pathways. It has allowed me to peek round corners hidden in the subconscious mind where the unknown lies shrouded in the mists of time. I have found that the entire history of humanity is recorded in the minds of people living today, and if these memories were undisturbed they would continue to lie dormant and undiscovered.

Yet circumstances created by our hectic modern world have caused these memories to come forth, often unbeckoned, because they influence present lifetimes in often inexplicable ways. Now that past-life therapy is being used as a tool to help solve problems, more of these memories are coming to light than ever before. People, perhaps for the first time, have allowed themselves to concede that the bodies they live in and the memories of their present lifetime are not the sumtotal of the human being. They are much more than what they see in the mirror and what they consciously remember. There are unfathomed depths that have only begun to be probed.

Since I began my work in 1979 I have found that we all apparently have memories of many past lives lying dormant in our subconscious. As long as we can function satisfactorily in our normal waking states, it is not important to explore these memories. I believe the most important lifetime of all is the one we are presently involved in, and that is our purpose for existing in the world at the present time. We must endeavor to live this life in the best way possible.

Many people argue that if reincarnation is a truth, and if they have lived countless other lives, why don't they remember them? The subconscious can be compared to a machine, a tape recorder, a highly advanced computer. In our present daily lives we are constantly being bombarded by millions of minuscule and mundane pieces of information: sights, smells, sounds, sensory input. If all this information were allowed through to our conscious mind, we could not function — we would be totally overwhelmed. Thus the subconscious acts as a filter and a guardian. It allows us to focus on the information we need in order to live and function in our society.

But it is important to remember that all the other data that has been collected is still there in the computer memory-banks. It is never lost, but stored away by a miser-type subconscious. Who knows the reason why? It is all there and can be tapped into. If a person were regressed to their twelfth birthday party in this lifetime, they could recall and actually relive the entire episode. They would know the names of all the children present, and if asked to do so, would even be able to describe the food, presents, furnishings and wallpaper, in detail. These are some of the mundane pieces of information that have been stored with the record of the birthday party. A complete recorded film and tape library exists in the mind to recreate the scene in minute detail. Every single day and event of our life is similarly recorded and can be accessed if necessary.

Thus if all our present life is available to the subconscious, all our former lifetimes are also there ready to be accessed. I like to compare it to a gigantic video tape library: we ask the subconscious to pull out the appropriate past life on videotape and insert it into the memory machine. If we realize the enormity of such a memory-bank, we can understand why it would not be wise — it would in fact be detrimental — for those memories to be conscious in our daily waking states. We would be overwhelmed. It would be extremely difficult to function if other scenes and former karmic relationships were constantly bleeding through and overlaying on to our lives now.

Thus the subconscious is selective in allowing us to focus upon what is most essential to living in our present situation and environment. Occasionally problems arise when former lifetimes influence the present life. Specific circumstances can often act as a trigger to bring a past life memory sharply into focus. This is the role of past life therapy: to help discover patterns that have been set up, or to deal with unresolved karma that is brought forward and is (often negatively) interfering with daily affairs.

Many of the people I and other past-life therapists have worked with have had years of professional help (physical and mental) without finding the answers they needed. Disturbing relationships with others, that have no explanation in this life, can often be traced to tense and traumatic events in other lives. Many phobias and allergies have their source in other lifetimes. As an example: an aversion to dust and dogs was traced to a lifetime of poverty when the subject, living in the desert, had to fight off dogs to protect a meager food supply. The origins of physical ailments that persist and resist conventional treatment can often be found in other lifetimes. A subject's long history of severe neck pains was traced to two violent deaths: one by guillotine and another by an Indian's tomahawk being buried in the back of the neck. A young college student could not complete his classes because severe abdominal cramps emerged during times of stress. This was traced back to several lifetimes where the death involved trauma to that part of the body: death by sword, being run over by a carriage, being shot, and so on. Compulsive over-eating and excessive weight gain can often result from lingering memories of a death from starvation, or by causing another to starve. The latter created a need for repayment of karmic debts.

A woman who desired to have a child, but experienced many miscarriages, discovered that she had died in childbirth in a past lifetime. Because the subconscious does not recognize the concept of time, it thinks it is performing its job of protection by not allowing this to occur again. Its method in the case of the woman who miscarried was to prevent any further pregnancy. In such cases therapy involves working directly with the subconscious and convincing it that the body that had the physical problems no longer exists, and the present body is perfectly healthy. Once it realizes the difference, and that the present personality is not at risk, the problems are quickly resolved.

Sometimes the answer can be found in a single past life. At other times the cause is more complex, because a pattern has been set up by repetition that spans several lifetimes. It is important to stress that, like all therapy, past-life work is not a magic cure-all. Once the clues are discovered the present personality still must use them as tools and incorporate the information into their present life. When the person applies the knowledge and works with it the results can be both startling and satisfactory.

Over the years that I have worked with hundreds and hundreds of subjects on a myriad of topics, there have occasionally been interesting cases that required more study. However, the vast majority of cases dealt with lifetimes that one would probably consider mundane and boring. It would appear that nothing interesting happened in them. But these are precisely the type of cases that add validity to past-life regressions. If, at some time in a future life, any of us were regressed to this present life, we would probably return to boring and ordinary scenes, because that is the way life *is*. Few of us are important enough or do anything sensational enough to get our names in the newspaper and on the TV news. There are many more ordinary people in the world than famous ones.

Even though I might consider a regression to be uneventful, the important point is that it helps the subject find what they are looking for. Many times after such a session, I thought the person would be disappointed. I was surprised when they said the memory was of extreme importance to them and explained something they had always wanted to know about. Thus I am not the one to judge which memories are important and useful as a therapeutic tool. These types of countless mundane regressions are the norm, and would never be written about unless it were as an accumulation of types of lives, or a condensed version of history as told by several people living in the same time-periods.

My books have come from the select few cases when I was fortunate enough to work with a subject who happened to be living in an important time in history, or was associated with an important personage. I have never yet discovered a Napoleon or a Cleopatra, and I do not expect to. The odds are more likely to find a lifetime where the subject was associated with Napoleon or Cleopatra. In such a case you would have to focus on their memories of that famous person, and you might never obtain any details more personal than that. Even if the person happened to live during an important historical event, they would only tell you what they personally knew. For example, the peasant would not be privy to the details known by the king of a country, and vice versa. The story would always be told from their unique viewpoint. Anything else would be immediately recognized as a fantasy.

When I wrote *Jesus and the Essenes,* I never thought I would ever encounter another subject who had knowledge of such personal details of the life of Christ. That book was the story as told by one of Jesus' Essene teachers at Qumran. It occurred when I regressed a young girl to that time period, and made the startling discovery. The girl had not even completed high school, and this made the Jewish historical and theological data even more important, because she had no way of compiling this information from her own education. But that case was a once-in-a-lifetime opportunity. This was why I spent so much time trying to obtain as many details as possible. The idea of ever encountering another subject who had lived in the same time period and who had also been associated with Jesus was remote.

I have regressed subjects to the time and the area, but they recounted normal lifetimes as a Roman soldier, a person living in Jerusalem, or someone selling wares in the market. They did not mention Christ, even though they probably were living in close proximity to him. This adds validity to my findings, because it shows that people are not prone to fantasizing the desire to have been associated with Jesus. When given the opportunity, they still told their own unique story. It is probably true that throughout the world there are a great number of people who had a past life with Jesus, and who carry this memory locked in their subconscious. But what were the odds of encountering any more of them in my work with regressive hypnosis? I would say the odds were slim, and justifiably so. I certainly did not expect it to happen again after my experience with Katie and the writing of that book in 1985.

I did work with a woman who was so convinced she had lived at that time, that she tried to fantasize a memory under hypnosis. I do not believe she was trying to be deceitful or had ulterior motives. She just strongly believed that she had been Elizabeth, the mother of John the Baptist, and no one was going to convince her otherwise. She wanted a regression to prove this to herself and her doubting family. I agreed to do a past-life regression with her, but I was not comfortable with it, and thus I was even more observant and diligent about monitoring the subject. As soon as she had gone into trance she began to describe the setting of the Holy Land, and her association with John and Jesus. She became very emotional as she talked about John's arrest and his impending death. There were several things that immediately disclosed that this was a fantasy. When I began to ask probing questions she could not answer them. She stuck strictly to the Biblical version and did not depart in any way. In other words, she could not answer any question that did not relate to what was available through reading the Bible.

Another clue was her bodily behavior. In normal trance the subject will lie almost motionless, while their breathing and muscle tone changes and REM (Rapid Eye Movement) increases. These are signs that are noticed by the hypnotist and are monitored to determine the depth of trance and also to alert any sign of trauma. This woman did not lie quietly. Her body displayed agitation. She was constantly wringing her hands, her breathing was erratic, and her eye-movements were not correct. Her entire demeanor displayed distress. After a half hour of this, during which time I was constantly using deepening techniques, she suddenly did what I call a "leap-frog." She jumped from the scene she was describing into a scene relating to a different life. This time she was an Italian priest of a small and poor church. Her body relaxed and a normal and mundane regression ensued. She told the story of a misfit priest who was very unhappy with the life fate had dealt him. I also relaxed because I knew we were once again upon solid ground. It was obvious what had happened. Her subconscious was trying to fulfil her wish and fantasize a lifetime with John and Jesus, but as the trance deepened it could no longer keep up the pretense and a normal regression came to light.

Another thing occurred during this session, which has happened on rare occasions. During the fictitious regression I felt an extreme amount of energy emanating from her body. When this happens it feels like heat, and creates a pulling, grasping effect on my body. It is most uncomfortable, and can disrupt my monitoring and concentration on questions. Often, if I can, I will move away from the subject (a few feet is often sufficient) until the sensation subsides. During this time that the woman's disturbing energy-flux was occurring, I noticed that the tape recorder had stopped running. While continuing to ask the subject questions I also tried to deal with this mechanical necessity to my work. When I opened it I found that the tape had jammed and was wound around the head. I pulled out a long stream of mangled twisted tape. I then inserted another tape and continued with the session. As she entered the normal regression of the Italian priest, the tape recorder operated smoothly. As I said, this has happened on rare occasions, and they were usually cases involving great tension and anxiety in the subject. Could the energy-field, which I could actually feel, somehow affect the tape recorder? I have also had cases when extreme static or noise will obliterate the voices on the tape. I believe this shows that there is more going on during past-life regression than we think. There appear to be invisible energies present and emanating from the people involved that can actually affect machinery, especially something as sensitive as a tape recorder.

When the woman awoke from trance, she was totally absorbed with her (supposed) memory of the lifetime with Jesus. She thought this was proof and dismissed the other lifetime of the priest. She was almost distraught when I told her the tape recording of that portion had been ruined. Besides the mangled tape, the wheels had jammed and the tape could not even be rewound. She begged me to somehow restore it because she had to have it. It was the most important thing in her life. This was another clue that the memory was not real, because a valid regression does not carry this type of reaction. The subject normally denies that the experience is real, saying they probably read it somewhere or saw it in a movie or on TV. Denial is the primary reaction, and it is normal for them to say, "Oh, I probably made the whole thing up." I believe this is the conscious mind's method of dealing with something so foreign and alien to its way of thinking. And past lives are certainly foreign to the average human's way of thinking. Thus I experienced a subject's innocent attempt at fantasizing a lifetime that would somehow fulfil her desire to have lived with these important historical personages. It was also further proof to me that these cases cannot be faked.

So I was not expecting to find any other subjects who had lived in the time of Christ, and if I did the former experience would make me highly suspicious. But these matters seem to be in the hands of others besides we mere mortals. The cases I am led to explore seem to come from higher sources that are certainly beyond my control. During 1986 and 1987, while I was heavily involved with the Nostradamus material (reported in my trilogy *Conversations With Nostradamus),* I had two subjects spontaneously regress to this time period, and my interest was again grasped. I have often wondered what the odds of this are, but I have since learned not to question the reasons, because I appear to be led inexplicably to the cases I am meant to report.

This book is the story of two women's separate encounters with Jesus in a past lifetime. Their memories add valuable pieces to the forgotten and distorted story that has come down to us through time. It helps us to better understand and appreciate this Jesus, who was foremost a man and a human being with complex and very real feelings and emotions. He was certainly a master teacher who understood the mysteries of the universe and attempted to reveal them to mortals of his time. As he said, "These things shall ye do and more." But he was also a human, and this is the part of his story that has been overlooked. In this book, as with *Jesus and the Essenes,* we have that rare opportunity to see him as the people of his own day saw him. It paints a picture of him that is deeply personal and real. Maybe at last the true Jesus can be seen and appreciated as the marvelous human that he was.

Enter the world of the unknown. The world of regression hypnosis.

Galilee at the time of Jesus

Chapter Two

A Meeting with Jesus

There are a variety of reasons for requesting a past-life regression session. Many people have a definite problem that they are attempting to resolve, whether it is physical or emotional. Karmic relationships with family members, or other significant people in their life, often cause problems that require help. These people have often exhausted conventional resources, both medical and psychiatric, and turn to past-life therapy as a possible solution. Then there are always those who request hypnosis for past lives purely out of curiosity, just to see if they did indeed live a former life.

When Mary called for an appointment, it was uncertain which category she belonged to. She was a very attractive woman in her late thirties. She was divorced and trying to raise two sons by herself. In order to do this she had started her own business, a small plant nursery and landscaping operation. Her schedule was busy and our sessions had to be worked in among her other appointments. She would arrive in her small van loaded with plants. After the session she would continue with her business deliveries. This was definitely not a bored housewife looking for an exciting outlet. Mary was a dedicated mother intent on making a success of her business so she could provide her two boys with the best possible home life.

She admitted she was searching for the answer to a problem, but she did not want to discuss what the problem was. She said simply that if we found it, she would recognize it. This meant that, as a therapist, I would be groping in the dark, not knowing what we were looking for. This can be remedied by allowing the subconscious free rein, and allowing it to find what the subject is looking for. So when we had our first appointment I put Mary into trance. I then allowed her to travel through time to wherever she wanted to go, without being directed to look for the cause of a problem.

I could easily predict what would happen, because these cases often follow a pattern. The results are usually the same. Mary went back to a lifetime that was mundane and boring, where little of significance happened. She said it answered some questions and related to things in her life, but had no connection to the major problem. The next week the results were the same, a normal past-lifetime that was only pertinent to Mary.

The breakthrough came during the third session. Mary was an excellent subject and I had conditioned her to go into deep trance by the use of a keyword. These keywords can be anything, and their use eliminates long inductions. After she had settled and relaxed on the bed I used her keyword and counted her down. After she had entered the deep trance state I requested her subconscious to provide information that was important for her to know about. I asked it to take her to a past-life that would have significance and relevance to her present lifetime. She was secure enough with me by this time that I hoped her subconscious would comply.

I perform so many sessions that I use several tape recorders. Often I just wear them out, both through recording and transcribing. The tapes of these sessions with Mary were made during a time my recorder was malfunctioning. I had held several sessions before I realized it was having trouble. It skipped at times and the wheels stopped turning on occasion. At these times I lost words. While transcribing these sessions I tried to recapture anything that was missing, as best as I could remember. Thus during these sessions I was often preoccupied with monitoring the tape recorder as well as the subject.

I was using a method where the subject is floating on a beautiful white cloud. I asked the cloud to deposit her in an important time where there was important information for her to know about.

I counted as the cloud carried her and let her down very gently. Her first impressions were that she was standing in a grove of green trees. She remarked that they had a smooth, slightly mottled grey bark that was unfamiliar to her. Then she

noticed a small group of four people among the trees. She could
see them from a distance, and they appeared to be dressed alike,
in white linen garments cinched at the waist by something like a
cotton rope belt. One woman had a linen kerchief covering her
hair. When Mary looked down at herself she discovered she
was dressed the same way, in a home-spun white linen garment
and sandals on her feet. She knew she was a young girl in her
teens with long brown hair. She said her name was Abigail, and
she had walked to this spot from a nearby village. I asked if she
wanted to go closer to the people.

"Yes", she answered. "I would like to know what they are
gathered for. Are they waiting for me to come? I must be the
shy one again, similar to the lifetime I am in now. Even now I
hesitate to join groups. Yes, I believe they're waiting for me."

Dolores: Do you know these people?
Mary: *Yes. I have been with them before. But I am the youngest
one. I don't know as much as they know.*
D: Are they neighbors or friends or what?
M: *I believe they are teachers. I have not spent a great deal of
time with them. I am feeling somewhat unworthy of their
teachings and attentions. It's hard for me to accept that
they would want me to be a student of theirs, because of
my age and because of their great wisdom. They seem to
be very wise, and I seem to be very young.*
D: I think it's very good that you want to learn.
M: *Yes.* (Laugh) *That is my nature. They have noticed my
eagerness. They believe that I am a worthy student, even
though I don't.*
D: Is it difficult to understand what they are teaching you?
M: *It's not difficult to understand. I am very privileged to be
able to know this information. These are spiritual
teachings that they have garnered over many years, and
need to pass on.*
D: How do they find their students?
M: *I believe my parents offered me forward. Where I am now,
it's as if the others are teachers and I am the only student.*
D: I think that would be difficult to have so many teachers.
M: *It is moral support. It is as if coming into a new family.
They are very warm and welcoming. They seem to be very
fond of me.*
D: Do you know what country we are in? Have you ever
heard anyone say?

M: (Long pause) *The word 'Palestine' comes to mind.*

D: Is it hot there?

M: *There's a breeze. It's warm out in the sun, but it's cool under the trees. It's a very pleasant location to learn. I like my studies with them. This is a very pleasant experience.*

D: Do you have to read or write?

M: *No, they teach by speaking. And I listen and learn and hold the knowledge in my mind, in my heart. I believe that I am to be a teacher. And that is why I will learn now at this age and I will be able then to teach as I become filled with wisdom.*

D: What kind of teachings are they giving you?

M: *Mysteries. That which is not known by most people.*

D: Well, many people wouldn't believe them anyway, would they?

M: *They don't care. They don't have the burning desire. That's why my parents offered me. They recognized that burning desire in me.*

D: You said you have not been a student with them very long?

M: *No. This maybe is my third meeting with them. We are getting to know one another, and learning personalities. It has a sense of something more special than teachers. It is almost a sense of coming into a family of aunts and uncles. As if they have been waiting for me, and now I am here. They have let me know that what they will share is called 'the mysteries', and that I will be very closely associated with them.*

D: Do you know where they learned this knowledge?

M: *They had teachers. It seems to reach back through time. These are as truths.*

These teachers sounded like Essenes, the same mysterious group that taught Jesus, although this was never definitely established. They certainly appeared to be members of a secretive Gnostic group that possessed knowledge that was not available to the general public.

I wanted to establish the time period, whether it was before or after the time of Christ, since the Essenes were active over a long time period. One method that worked in *Jesus and the Essenes* was to ask about the Messiah.

D: Has the Messiah come yet to your country, or do you know?

M: (Pause) *The Messiah?*

D: Have you ever heard that word?

M: *The Messiah? It seems as if that is something that will someday be. I don't know of that.*

D: Are there Jewish people where you live? People that study the Jewish religion?

M: (Long pause) *It doesn't seem to be pertinent.*

D: Because I believe it's part of their beliefs that a Messiah will come someday. That's why I wondered if you had heard those stories.

M: *It doesn't seem to... The knowledge doesn't seem to be there.*

D: Alright. I was just trying to determine what time we are in. And time is sometimes very difficult to understand. Is there a ruler of your country — do you know that?

In *Jesus and the Essenes* time was calculated by the number of years of the ruler's reign. But this was of no help in this case.

M: *No, I don't know that. I was raised in a small community. It's almost as if my whole life has been waiting for this time. Outside influences have not been part of my understanding. I seem to have lived a very sheltered life, very protected. We have a community, a small village. I know the village people, but nothing of the larger world. As if I was being kept untouched, so that when the time came for the teachings I would be almost as virgin material.*

D: So you wouldn't be influenced in any way by the outside world.

M: *I believe that is a true statement.*

D: I can understand that. Have you had any other teachings before this time?

M: *My parents. They are very gentle people. My life in the village has been very peaceful. A wonderful childhood. My mother makes some kind of flat cake bread that I like very much. She cooks this over a griddle. They seem to be a favorite of mine.* (She abruptly stopped reminiscing). *But now I am no longer a child. And it is time for me now to enter a new part of my life, and to put away those fond memories.*

D: But at least you do have the fond memories. Do you have any brothers or sisters?

M: (Pause, then surprised) *Oh! It looks as if there is a small sister. She and I are very fond of each other.*

D: I was thinking, aren't you at the age that you would be marrying?

M: *Well, I don't believe that is what I am called to do. I am very happy to be a student now. That is something I have been waiting for, and looking forward to. Each of these people will have a different role in teaching me, in my learning. They will each share in my education. It seems that...* (pause)

D: What is it?

M: *It seems that there will be thorough preparation for public service, as in a temple.*

D: Then you will have many things to learn, won't you?

M: *Yes. Broad, broad understanding. Spiritual base. Truth.*

D: Will you be able to pass on to me what you are being taught?

M: *Well, I don't know that now, because I don't know what these teachings are. I have no hesitation in sharing, once it becomes known to me.*

It was evident that the teaching would go on for quite a long time, so I decided to move the story forward. I usually do this by asking the subject to go ahead in that lifetime to an important day. Since most lives are mundane and are filled with simple ordinary daily routine (as our present lives are), this is the most effective method to locate an important focal point, if one exists. There have been lifetimes where the subject could find nothing that was significant, which again rules out fantasy. When I finished counting Mary (as Abigail) ahead in time, her facial and body sensations showed that something was occurring. I asked her what was happening. There was no answer, but from her definite physical reactions, and her deep sighs, I knew it was something disturbing.

D: What are you experiencing?

M: *I seem to be... older. My teachers are no longer with me.*

D: Did you study a long time with them?

M: *Yes. Fourteen years.*

D: Where are you?

M: (Pause) *I seem to be... at a temple. There is... something is*

not... all is not well.
D: What is the matter?
M: (Long pause) *I believe that I am not being allowed to teach. It's as if my mind is full, and there is a constricting band around my head. I am not being allowed to share. It's... my people. It's as if I have been... put away.*
D: But you have so much knowledge, why wouldn't they allow you to teach? You have many important things to pass on.
M: *They are not happy about the knowledge that I have.*
D: Who are they?
M: *The elders. The men. I am a woman. They say women are not worthy to be taught anything. I am not to have this kind of knowledge. They don't want me to teach.* (Painfully) *My head!*

When the subject is experiencing real physical sensations, I always remove these. These can be reported from an objective viewpoint rather than by actually reliving any pain or discomfort. This keeps the subject comfortable and lets them know I will always take care of them. It also helps them to relate the story without the distraction of physical sensations. I gave her suggestions for well-being. I then attempted to gain her confidence, so she would be able to tell me the things she could not express to others.

D: You can talk to me even if you can't talk to the others. Have you been teaching before this time?
M: *Children. I taught... children would be brought to me. And I would share with them. The parents would bring them. We would sit on the steps of the Temple. And we would learn by playing games and telling stories and dancing. And I would bring light into their minds.*
D: Oh, I think that's a very wonderful way to teach, because it's hard for a child to understand sometimes. I would love it if you could share some of those things with me, as though I was a child. For there may be things that I don't know, and I am very eager to learn. How did you teach them?
M: *We had a bird. A little white... ah, like a pigeon. Very beautiful...* (she had a sudden revelation) *a turtle dove. The turtle dove was a special... oh, a friend of mine. The turtle dove and I were very close. And I would use the dove as*

an example for the children. I brought the dove in the cage, and then showed the children the cage door was open. The dove could walk out and look around and see new faces, and have a larger space in which to roam. And indeed, to take wing and fly. I was showing them that all children have this opportunity, this chance, this doorway that opens unto a much larger understanding. And that if they come to me and spend time with me, they start to understand the world is much larger than their little cages. And that their spirits can expand into this space. There is nothing between them and flight. That they too can fly and be supported by the winds of the spirit. Ascend higher and higher. And come back, come back to the people that are in this earthier place. And they can say to these, 'Come, look what I have found! Come, fly with me!' And then take someone with them.

D: That's very beautiful.

M: *Oh, the turtle dove is a wonderful, wonderful spirit-friend.*

D: I like that, because I can understand it too.

M: *Oh, yes. There's so much more out there than you can ever imagine. The children are so precious.*

D: What else did you show them?

She shifted from remembering the event to experiencing it, as though she moved to that scene.

M: *There's something red lying over on the step* (she seemed to be studying it). *It seems to be two pieces of wood. Cylindrical. They're lying there... waiting to be used.*

D: What are they used for?

M: (A revelation) *Oh! They're used for rhythm. They're used for percussion.* (Smiling broadly) *They're used to keep time as the children dance. Let me see.* (Pause, as though watching).

D: What's happening?

M: (Laugh) *Oh, we dance up and down the steps. The steps are very broad and spacious. They are deep and are very long. This is just a wonderful spot.* (Surprised) *It's not unlike the grove. Ahhh! As the pillars and the overhang...* (merry laugh) *the shadow, the cool, but the sunshine just on the other side. The children are very happy to come here. They have a lot of space. And they have their time with me. It's a very special time for all of us. We learn through dancing, as we go in and out, and circle around.*

D: What kind of lesson could be taught with the dancing?

M: *The importance of a physical expression of their inner emotions. Of allowing what is in them to become manifest in action. And as we now learn simple rhythms, simple patterns, simple steps that bring release and joy, and are accompanied by rhythm and music. We use a tambourine also. They will be able to learn, at this tender age, those ways to express what they will be required to use when they are older and themselves teaching. They must stay in touch with expression. They are encouraged not to hold it all in, but to give it voice, to give it action. To see a pattern and to know there's a goal. This is all held in the very simple beginnings of this little dance. It's a pattern they learn now, and it will enable them to carry that into their adult life when it's not so easy to express spontaneously some patterns, some actions. They will be able to recall, how in their youth, there was spontaneity. They will remember the joy that produced in them, that freedom, that happiness. There's such **joy** in God's word. There's such **joy** in His spirit. As His spirit moves through and is manifest in action, it is a very joyful experience.*

D: It sounds as if it is. I think you are a very good teacher.

M: *Oh, thank you.*

D: You have very good methods.

M: (Happily) *Thank you.*

I got the impression she was not used to receiving compliments for her work.

D: What city are we in now? Where is this temple?

M: *Jerusalem.*

D: Do they have a name for the type of teachings that you do? I am thinking of an organization or a group that you might be a member of.

M: *I seem to be... solitary.*

D: What does that mean?

M: *I am not associated. I seem to be... **attached** to the Temple. That is where I sleep. My needs are met through my service in the Temple.*

D: It sounds as if this is a large temple.

M: *Yes, it is a large temple. Open, tall columns, altars.*

D: What religion is the temple to?

M: (Pause) *I believe Jewish.*

This was further indication that she was associated with another group. Was it the Essenes?

D: You were talking about God's words, so I wondered what god you worshiped.
M: *Well, my understanding is different from the understanding of the men. As long as I deal with the children I am humored. I am to keep silence in my understandings.*
D: I can't see anything wrong with them.
M: *The priests...* (she hesitated — it was difficult to explain). *It is very distasteful to me. Their behavior, their teachings. They are so* **closed**. *They are so* **dark**. *They are not of the light. They are not of the* **truth** *even. They keep people away from the* **immediacy** *of our experience with God. He's not somewhere* **far off** *that is so hard to get to. He's not* **angry** *at us. He doesn't require us to kill beautiful animals as a sacrifice. He is* **with** *us, in every breath we take. He is* **part** *of us. He lives within us.* **We are God** *in physical form.* **We are It.** *It's not some* **thing** *far away that we cannot attain to. We are not unworthy rabble. We are* **each** *holy, each given these beliefs, and we have that essence of holiness. It's just* **so covered up** *that it can't shine forth.* (This was all said quietly but with much emphasis.) *It is frustrating. I have a sense of having so much understanding and not being able to teach.*
D: Maybe this is why I have come. You can teach me and it will help you, so you won't feel so restricted. But the priests are teaching people these other beliefs?
M: *It sounds very exalted. Very far above the common people. As if the common people cannot get to God directly without the priests. It is their part, but it keeps the people away from knowing that God is in them.*
D: Are you the only woman teacher?
M: *I am the only one. I have some kind of service. The children seem to be an acceptable way to get me out of the mainstream, and into an appropriate woman's place.*

When I later did my research I discovered that in Jesus' time there was no requirement of attendance at any school. If a Jewish male child received education, the only schools were connected with the synagogues, and the only schoolbooks were the Hebrew Scriptures. To the Jews *knowledge* meant "knowledge of the Law of Moses", or the Torah. Nothing else was taught, and *education* meant merely "education in religion". Anyone who understood "the Law" thoroughly and had the facility to explain it, provided he chose to teach, was regarded as "a learned man": a Rabbi. Adherence to the strict letter of the Law was regarded as a prominent characteristic of the learned men of the time.

We discovered in *Jesus and the Essenes* that there was a very strong male chauvinist attitude (as we now know it) in Palestine at that time. Women had highly-defined roles, and any deviation from these was not accepted. They were not educated, and had their own section in a temple, so as not to mix with men during worship. Abigail's case is not a contradiction with these rules, because she indicated that she was not Jewish. She had to have been educated by another group that was not bound by these regulations. The Essenes had no such restrictions, and taught everyone according to their own desire and ability to learn.

It must have deeply irritated the men priests to find that Abigail had not only been educated, but *vastly* trained in fields they were unfamiliar with. This they could not abide. It could not be allowed.

It was never made clear why Abigail was assigned to a place where she was unwelcome. Apparently the men did not want her there, but they could not remove her. Their only solution was to put her in a position where she would pose no threat to them with her superior knowledge and different way of thinking. They placed her in a woman's role, taking care of the children, where they thought she could cause no damage. They were wrong. She soon devised a way to teach, a method to pass knowledge on discreetly to the children under the disguise of play. But the real knowledge could not be imparted, and her head ached from this. As she said, it was as if a tight band was around her head, and she felt as though her mind would explode from the pressure of the information wanting release.

D: Did you study the traditional Jewish teachings also?
M: *They don't seem to be in my mind.*
D: Have you ever heard of the story of the Messiah?
M: (Pause) *I don't know of the Messiah, but I believe there is a man teaching. He is not happy with the priests either*

(sigh). *I believe there is a man with an understanding similar to mine.* (Pause) *The kingdom of God is within. The temples are not to separate God from man. The temples are to be a place of union. Man should be able to come into the holy space, and invite God directly into his heart. Not through sacrifices, not through intercessions, but be allowed to stand on that holy ground and commune directly with God.*

D: I agree with you. But this other man, have you ever seen him or heard him speak?

M: *I believe he's been at a different location on the Temple steps than where I teach. It is as if it is a rectangle. I would teach the children on the long side of the building. He has stood on the narrow end, as you approach the Temple.*

D: Have you heard him when he was talking to the people?

M: *I believe he was speaking to a crowd when I had the children on the other side of the stairs.*

She again shifted from past tense to present, indicating she went to that time to relive the incident and report.

M: *He speaks with much authority. I am curious to know who this is.*

D: Have you heard anyone say who he is?

M: *This is most unusual. There is a man motioning to us to come. The children and I. He says, 'Come! You must hear him. This man is the son of God'.*

D: Is he also on the steps?

M: *He's running toward the end where the crowd is gathered.*

D: Are you going to go with him?

M: *I am torn between going to hear this person speak — I cannot leave the children unattended. They... I do not think... I am not willing for them to come with me at this time. I do not know what it is that I would be taking them to. And I am very careful with the children.*

D: I think you're very wise because you don't want to endanger the children. Do you stay with them instead of going to see who this man is?

M: *I am torn. I am as halfway between each.*

D: I suppose you're very curious, too.

M: *Yes. I want to know who this is that speaks with such authority.*

D: Can you hear him speaking?

M: *I can hear his voice. He speaks with complete authority. (Laugh) Ah! I must return to the children. They are my responsibility.*

D: But at least you can hear him from where you are.

M: *He's a distance away. I can hear speaking, I cannot discern words. I can discern his tone of voice. He speaks very clearly.*

D: Maybe you will find out someday who he is, and be allowed to hear him, and see him up close.

I was trying to bring this session to a close. Before we began this day's work Mary had said she wanted to come out of trance at a certain time because she had an appointment. If Abigail wasn't going to go over and hear this man, we would probably not be able to learn much more at this time. I did not know if the man was Jesus, but the indications were leading in that direction. I wanted to pursue this and find out. I didn't want to get involved now because I wanted to devote more time to this event, and both time and tape were running out. I planned to continue in the next session.

M: *I have a feeling that we will know each other. There is a common understanding that will draw us to each other. I can be patient.*

D: Yes, this is true, people who think alike will usually find each other. But I was curious about the Jewish beliefs that someday a Messiah will come. Is it true that they are looking for a Messiah, do you know?

M: *It's as if... I will not carry that in my mind. It's as if what I have in my mind is light, is pure. And it is as if I will not accept anger, fear, condemnation. I will not carry it in my mind.*

She had deliberately shut out or perhaps had not been exposed to any of the traditional Jewish theology. She apparently had been very sheltered. In the beginning of the session she said she was as virgin material when her teachers began their classes. Maybe this was intentional, so she would not be influenced by traditional schools of thought.

D: Then you are not accepting any of the men's teachings.

M: *I seem to have some kind of shield around me that... I*

don't accept it in my mind.

D: I can see why you would block it out, because the men are so negative, even though they're supposed to be priests of God.

M: **Pompous**, *if you'll forgive me. This man has light around him. That's why I know that I will know him someday.*

D: Can you see him?

M: *Yes, I can see that there is light around him.*

D: Did you go around the building?

M: *No. I can see through the columns. He's at a different location, but I can see. Yes, he is of the light.*

D: Do you normally see lights around people?

M: *Children sometimes, but not as this light. This light has white light all around him.*

D: Oh, that must be very beautiful.

M: *Well, it sets him off from others* (laugh).

D: (Laugh) Can you see what he looks like, or is he too far away?

M: *He's at a side-angle to me. He seems to be in white with some kind of brown cinched at the... it's as if there is a piece of cloth that goes over his shoulders, front and back, and then it's held next to his body at the waist.*

D: Can you see what his features look like?

M: *No, he's distant. We are of like mind. It's almost as if there is a... connection, even at this distance.* (She let out a sudden gasp.)

D: What is it? (Another intake of breath). What is it?

M: *Oooh! Yes, he felt the connection.*

D: What?

M: *He is coming! He is coming! He is coming up the stairs. To see the children!* (Her voice was in complete awe).

And I was running out of tape! I could not put another one in the machine because of the restrictions Mary had placed on the sessions. What bad timing, to have something like this happen at this point. Frustrated, I knew I would have to find some way to close the session without upsetting her, so we could return to it next time for closer examination in more detail.

M: *The crowd is following him. He perceives the light around the children. He understands. We are of like mind.*

D: Well, this is very beautiful, but I'm afraid we're going to have to leave it. I would love to hear it, but we're running out of time. I can't stay with you today. Can you return to it again if we leave this?

M: *Oh, I would like very much to know more about this man.*

D: Then the next time I come we will continue with this. It's very beautiful and I appreciate you sharing it with me. Now let us leave that scene.

She was still making sounds of awe and delight. I really hated to do this, but we had no alternative. She had obligations to attend to in the "real world".

D: Carry the beautiful feeling with you. Let's drift away from that scene, and we shall return to it another time. Carry the beauty of it and the warmth and the love with you, as you drift away from that scene.

Her facial expressions and body movements were displaying protest. She really didn't want to leave the scene, but she had to obey the instructions given by me, the hypnotherapist. She could not remain in trance, no matter how much she wanted to. The scene was evaporating, and she was being pulled forward through time and returning to the room.

D: It's all right. We shall come back to it, I promise.

I oriented her personality to the present time and then brought Mary back to full consciousness. When she awakened she was still under the spell of that closing scene. She began crying. I apologized for having to take her away from it. She understood because she was the one who had set the time-limits for the session, but she was still disappointed. I quickly put in a fresh tape, and recorded part of her conversation after awakening:

D: I just want to record a little of what you said. You said that as you looked in each other's eyes it was love at first sight?

M: *There was a depth of understanding that was overwhelming. I couldn't believe that I was being asked to leave. I mean, I had just **gotten** there. It was so **strong**.*

D: Sorry! (Laugh)

M: *Dolores, it was like things that have happened to me in this lifetime that I haven't been able to understand. I have* been taken away *from things that mean so much.* (With resolution:) *But we 'll go back.*

D: We will, and then we'll be able to finish it. But you weren't close enough, I guess, to really....

M: *I was almost close enough to reach out and touch his hand.*

D: Could you get a look at his face?

M: *Yes.* (In awe) *I was looking in his eyes.*

D: What did his face look like?

M: *Oooh! Strong... and gentle... and love. That was all that was on his face... was* **love***. His eyes were... there was just love. He was not big.* **So** *gentle.* **So** *kind. Oooh, we 've* **got** *to go back.*

D: What color hair did he have?

M: (Pause) *Almost as if when the sun hit it there was some red in it.*

D: Did you see the color of his eyes?

M: *No. They were very deep eyes. The eyes were almost as if there was no end to them. They just went straight on... straight on inside.* (Laugh) *It was like that saying, how you 'get lost in somebody's eyes'. That was what it was like. The children were very excited. They could see that there was something going on here. And they didn't know who to look at* (laugh).

D: I have never had to leave a scene at a worse spot (laugh). I normally plan it better than that, so this confusion and dissatisfaction can be avoided.

I did not know much about Mary's private life. As she sat on the edge of the bed, she now confided that she had been married and divorced three times. She said that all during her life things and people she loved had been taken away from her. And that was how she felt about this. Right at the point when she saw him (apparently a high point in her drab unhappy life), I made her leave. She was very impressed by this man and wanted to know more about him. From her descriptions and reactions, there was no doubt in my mind that the man she had seen was Jesus. This was why I was very surprised when she said, with a faraway look in her eyes, "I wonder who he was."

Startled, I asked, "You mean you don't know?" She said she really didn't have any idea, except that he was definitely a remarkable and unusual man. I replied that I didn't think I would tell her my assumptions, and I would let her find out for herself during the next session. Her remarks would seem to definitely rule out any unconscious desire on her part to create a fantasy trip that would allow her to meet Jesus. She did not even recognize him as that person.

She gathered her belongings, and with a heavy sigh entered her van. She then returned to the everyday business world of delivering her plants.

The scene she described clung to me and permeated the air around me with a soft sweetness. Yes, we would return. I had to know more about this remarkable man she had brought forth through time.

Chapter Three

The Healing

It was upsetting both to Mary and myself when I had to end the last session abruptly at such a crucial point. When we met the next week I was determined to return to the same day, if it were possible. Hopefully we could continue with the story of Abigail's encounter with the unusual man whom I recognized as Jesus.

Before we began the session Mary wanted to tell me about her memory of the dance with the children on the Temple steps. We sat on the couch and I turned on the tape recorder. In working with these cases it is never wise to attempt to rely on your memory or notes, as too many details may be lost that may prove invaluable later. A chance insignificant remark may turn out to be an important link that will tie the story together. The tape recorder is an indispensable tool, even though weeks will often pass before the tapes can be transcribed.

The faraway look in Mary's eyes was evidence that she was visually reliving the scene in her mind. She once again saw the children on the steps, laughing and carefree.

M: *The way it came into my visual memory was that the children and I would start in a single-file line, and we would curve around and turn ourselves into a little tight circle. And then the leader would lead us out of that tight circle into the open again. We'd do a little curve around, come back into a little tight circle, and then we'd undo it again* (all this was accompanied with hand motions). *The purpose of this was to symbolically explain to the children that there were times in our lives when we needed to go into ourselves and be quiet and alone. And then a time to go into the world and be out and open. Then the next balance would be back into yourself, to be by yourself and alone, and then again out into the world. It was used as an example or an understanding for them to know the balance between the contemplative life and an active life. I could see the symbolic meaning. It came through as clear as a crystal to me.*

D: You said you also used some type of sticks and a tambourine.

M: *Yes, that was for percussion, and was a different dance. That one wasn't as clear to me, except that I could see the children on the steps. There must have been a wide step that was a breakdown between two staircases where we did that dance. The steps of the Temple weren't like one set of stairs. It was like a set of stairs and then a wide landing, and then another set of stairs. So I think we did that kind of dance on the wide landing.*

D: At first it sounded strange that you were dancing on the steps. But they weren't like we think of as stairs.

M: *They were very wide. I was teaching the children this way. And the men felt this was safe, because they thought I couldn't influence the children. I was in my 'appropriate' place. But there was much spiritual teaching done. I'll tell you another interesting thing that occurred this summer, that was very uncharacteristic of me. I was at a large garden supply place here in town that I use for my business. I'd gone in there to pick up plants to install in a commercial garden that I was doing. And all of a sudden I saw this little pottery piece that was shaped like a dove, sitting down there on the floor. And for some reason I could **not** take my attention off that dove. I finally bought it. The reason it was so uncharacteristic is because it cost $34, and that's a lot of money to pay for a pottery dove (laugh). But it was as though that dove spoke to me. I mean, it was an **instant** reaction. And last week during the regression, when that dove came out of her cage, I almost said, 'Paloma', because that was what I named the little pottery piece.*

D: That is the Spanish word for dove. But that dove must have been trained, because it didn't fly away.

M: *Right. She and I had a spiritual connection. We communicated.*

D: I thought when you let it out, it would fly away. But apparently it stayed right there.

M: *She flew. She circled around. She showed all the freedom of flight. She knew to exhibit her freedom in the sky, and she knew to come back, so that she could teach others how to go and fly.*

D: That was the symbolism.

M: *She really understood that she was a spiritual aid in my teaching. We were* **very** *close.*

D: And that incident with the pottery dove occurred months before we started to work. Maybe your subconscious was trying to set you up for this, as if saying 'this is time' or something. Seeing the little statue was trying to trigger a memory.

M: *Well, it must have. Because when I got home that night after the regression, and I walked past Paloma, I thought, 'Now I understand why you are so dear to me'.*

D: It was an important connection to a memory.

As we began the regression, my task was to return Mary to the same lifetime and hopefully locate the same scene again. I used her keyword and counted her back to the lifetime of Abigail.

D: I will count to three and we will go back through time and space. On the count of three we will be at the time when Abigail lived in Jerusalem. 1... 2... 3... we have gone back through time and space to the time that Abigail was in Jerusalem. What are you doing? What do you see?

When I finished counting Mary displayed facial reactions.

D: What is it?

M: (Smiling) *The children. Can you see the children? I'm so close to the children. They are so dear to me.*

D: What are the children doing?

M: (Laugh) *Being children. Bouncing around. Climbing up and down the stairs. They're just being joyful. Talking to the turtle dove.*

D: Oh, they like that turtle dove, don't they?

M: *Yes. She's such a special spirit.*

D: Where are you?

M: *On the steps of the Temple.* (Very loving tone of voice:) *Children are so special. One little girl likes the tambourine. We have ribbons coming off the side of it. And she loves to dance around and shake the tambourine, and let those ribbons stream. We're not trying to do a structured learning thing right now. We're just spending time together.*

D: Didn't you say that the priests will let you work with the children?

M: *Yes, yes. Unbeknownst to the priests, these children are vessels. They are repositories for the knowledge and training that I have been given. And whether the children fully understand what we are doing during our time together, it still becomes a part of them. And when their life gets to a point when that information can be helpful to them, they will be able to pull it out. They will have that pattern established.*

D: They may not remember where it comes from, but it will be there.

M: *Right. We have such influence over the lives of the children as they develop. It's almost as a conditioning to them at this age. We influence how they respond to their world as they get older. If you prepare them in the ways of understanding and wisdom, they will be able to pull that out of their memory in their later lives.*

D: And the priests think you can do no harm this way.

M: *I'm safe. I'm doing something that is safe, and acceptable work for a woman. Allowing the children to be around the Temple, and letting them have a woman who is not an intimidating figure to them. Yes, my work is... oh, it's just a crumb that they have thrown to me, not knowing what an opportunity they have given me.*

D: It's probably something they didn't want to be bothered with.

M: *Yes. And they do understand that women have a certain way with children, that they themselves do not have. They are so filled with their own importance and position that they can't help but intimidate children. It's almost as if they strike fear in the hearts of children* (distastefully). *Because of their elaborate costumes, their headpieces and robes, and all the paraphernalia that goes along with that function , that role. So here the children and I play in our everyday clothes. We can sit in the sun, and we can move to the shade if it gets too warm. And we have common easily-loved tools to work with, because our life is a common life. Very few people get into positions of unusual authority or have elaborate support systems around them. We all live in common everyday ways. And if we can take the common tools of our lives, and understand that they can represent a much larger understanding, then we have accomplished something in the lives of regular people.*

D: We have more influence than we realize we do.

M: *Yes, I think that is true. I think we do not fully appreciate how much we can influence the children around us.*

D: I think the priests are making a mistake. You could be a big help to the adults, too, but they don't realize that.

M: (Softly) *The knowledge. I don't know where the knowledge is going to go.*

D: Well, you're doing your part by helping these children.

M: *Yes, this simple preparatory. But the full knowledge that I have is... I don't know, maybe somebody will be brought to me that I can pass it on to. My head is so full. My head... I do what I can do.*

D: There is always me. I am eager to learn, and I appreciate what you are doing.

M: *Thank you.*

D: But if the priests don't want you there, why are you there? I thought maybe they could chase you out or make you leave. Can't they do that?

M: *My understanding is that I am attached. That part was arranged by the people that I trained with. This was the goal or the outcome of that teaching and preparation. When it was completed, I was to go to the Temple. This was supposed to be an excellent place for me to teach and share the knowledge. They didn't know this would happen. It wasn't supposed to be this way, but nothing can be done about it now. The priests understand that I have mystical knowledge, and they think this is not to be shared with the common people. Nor am I to be in a position of influence as a teacher. It is as if they have effectively bottled up what I have been given. They allow me only a very minor outlet, and that is with the children. But the children are such a small part of what I have been prepared to do. I'm not being allowed to do what I was prepared to do. That's why my mind... my head is so tight, so full.*

D: I think the priests are probably afraid of you. They want it all their own way.

M: *Yes. I think that even though these men have set themselves up to be spiritual leaders, they go by the letter of the Law of the Books. They have no use for knowledge, or for that which comes into the heart as a gift of God, but only what can be read from the written page. And the knowledge that has been shared with me and that I must share with others, is of an esoteric nature. They have no use for it. They are somewhat frightened, but more than that — they just don't understand it as a complement to the Law* (she was referring to the Torah, or book of Jewish rules of conduct). *They see it as a frivolous, almost formless, aspect of spirituality. I believe they think it is properly* **contained** *in a woman's mind, because it is of feeling and intuition and spirit-knowing, rather than the mind, the reasoning. Oh, their rules!*

D: What kind of rules?

M: *They have a rule for* **everything***. Look it up in the Book, instead of looking into the heart. They lose the* **spirit** *of the Law, as they look to the* **letter** *of the Law.*

D: I don't think they would understand even if you tried to explain it to them. They aren't the proper type of people.

M: *I agree.*

D: But I hope that if we meet like this you can share some of your esoteric knowledge with me. I'd be grateful to learn these things. It may help you to release it in that way.

M: *At this time... that seems not acceptable.*

D: I didn't mean right at this minute. I meant sometime.

M: *You would have to go through... as an initiation or an introduction, for you to understand what it is you're asking to receive. Then you would decide whether you indeed wanted the responsibility of this knowledge. As I say, the carrying of this knowledge without release is a physical pain in my head. It is from here to here, a physical pain* (she made motions across the width of her forehead).

D: Across your forehead. Well, I don't want you to be uncomfortable.

M: *I am used to it. It is there.*

D: (I gave suggestions to alleviate any actual physical

sensations). While I speak to you it won't bother you. I don't want you to be uncomfortable in any way.

M: *Thank you.*

D: But maybe as we work together and I visit with you, you might be able to give me the initiation and we could find out.

M: *It will be up to you. It is a responsibility that is not taken lightly.*

D: Alright. But today I'm interested in what you are doing. You're playing with the children. Are there any other people around?

M: *It seems there are people that are rather wandering around. They don't seem to have a focused purpose or specific aim to their walk. More like visiting, looking around, seeing what it is like. Maybe they are from outside our area, and live away from here. So this would be a special opportunity for them to come into this space and acquaint themselves with this Temple. They look up and say, 'Oh, look!'* (pointing).

D: Is the Temple beautiful?

M: *Yes, it is very big. Tall, high spaces. It is an... I hesitate to use the word 'intimidating', but the size is remarkable.*

D: This is probably what they are amazed about. Well, on this day, is anything else happening right there around the Temple?

I was trying to return to the encounter with the man I assumed to be Jesus, and continue that story. I didn't know if this was the same day or not.

M: (Softly) *That man!*

D: What man?

M: *That man of light.*

Apparently she was seeing him once again. We had returned to the same scene without asking to. However, this was our intention, and Mary's subconscious was aware of this.

D: The last time I spoke to you, you could see him through the columns, and he was speaking to some other people with a voice of authority. Is that what you see?

Her facial expressions were those of a pleasant experience.

M: *Yes. That light.*
D: What does the light look like?
M: *It is white.* **Completely** *around him. It emanates from every part of his body. From his feet... all,* **all** *around his body... to his head* (amazed). *It's as if he walks in a capsule of light.*
D: Oh, it sounds beautiful.
M: *It's most remarkable. I've never seen anything like that. He is of the light.*
D: What do you think is causing the light?
M: *His spirit. It is an outer manifestation of his* **inner** *light. It simply cannot be contained in a physical body, and so it emanates out. It is really clear, just for me to see.*
D: Are you surprised that you can see something like that?
M: *Oh, no, no, that's not uncommon. Just the* **nature** *of the light itself is most unusual. It is such a white light.*
D: You mean it's not unusual for you to see lights around people.
M: *No, no, I am of that knowledge.*
D: Were the other lights you've seen different?
M: *Yes. This is very different. The children, you see, have their soft glows about them. Their pinks and their yellows and their greens. Very soft childlike glowing jewels. This man is a diamond. This man is a clear white powerful light. Very, very powerful.*
D: What is he doing?
M: *He is talking to people. He's using his arms as he talks. He does speak with much authority. He's not necessarily pleased with the behavior of some people.*
D: Can you hear him saying these things?
M: *No, I can tell by the tone of his voice. His words are not clear to me. He's facing another direction, and the projection is away from my hearing. But the tone of voice tells much.*
D: As though he's not pleased about something.
M: *Well, it's not a reprimand. It's more of a... an explanation. A very firm explanation. If they can see the truth, then they will be able to align themselves more with his light.*
D: This is difficult for people to do.
M: *Those people that are standing around him seem to be of a*

very dark and dense energy. It's almost as if... (an intake of breath, a revelation) *it's almost as if he's talking to lumps of coal!* (laugh). *They seem really dark and dense. And he has such a light. He seems to be trying to allow them to come out of their denseness, and receive some of his light. And he's using firm language to get their attention, and help them understand the importance of what he is saying. It is not unkind. It is, as they say, gentle but firm.*

D: Sometimes that's what you have to have.

M: *Yes. This man is very loving. It's as if he loves all those lumps of coal* (laugh). *And he wants so much...* (another intake of breath, another revelation). *Oooh! He wants to turn them into diamonds. That's why the analogy is there. Those lumps of coal can become diamonds like himself.* (She was very pleased by her discovery).

D: It would take a great deal of work though, wouldn't it ?

M: *Oh, they are so dense. They are so dark. He has quite an undertaking.*

D: Would you want to go and listen to him?

M: *I feel as if I can wait. As long as the children are in my care I will keep their little spirits joyful and safe, secure, so that they always feel almost as if they are in a protective cocoon when they are with me. I think it enhances the teachings. I think they are more receptive to having the teachings settle into a deep part of their mind, when we maintain that cocoon around us, as a unit, as a body, as the teacher and students are one.*

D: The last time you spoke of this I thought you were afraid to take them there. Because you didn't know who this man was and what he was saying, that maybe it might frighten the children.

M: *There was that man who said, 'Come and listen'. I will stay with the children. Our relationship is very important, and I don't want there to be intrusion upon that. It's almost as if we stay in a sphere of colored light as we are together. Yes, I will stay here and we will maintain. But I can see that this gentleman would not be an intrusion. Rather* **his** *light would expand to encompass* **our** *light.*

D: I thought maybe there was fear there, that you thought the children would be endangered in some way.

M: *No, it's more a matter of maintaining our own sphere. You know when you get around those black lumps of coal it can't help but affect your own aura, your own glow and light.*

D: Yes, I can understand that.

M: *And the children are with me in a trust bond. I have no desire to take them around that other energy. They will have plenty of that in their lives. We have a trust relationship. I will maintain that.*

D: That is good. It was not him that you were worried about being around.

M: *I don't think I have to fear that man.*

D: I'm going to move ahead a little bit. Last time you said he sensed your presence and turned around?

M: *Yes! It's almost as if there is a connection between us. A bond that can travel through this physical space. It's almost as if we are **attracted** to each other. That the energy within him and the energy within me are similar energies, and we are pulled to that light energy.*

D: Tell me what is happening.

M: *He senses my presence, because he is sensitive to energy.*

D: It must be a different type of energy from the ones he's speaking to.

M: *Yes, yes* (chuckling).

D: (Long pause) What is he doing now?

M: *He is still talking to the other people.* (Long pause)

Her facial expressions indicated that she was experiencing something.

D: What is it?

M: (Softly) *Yes, he... he will come.*

D: What do you mean?

M: (Sounds of delight) *He will come. In response to our light.*

D: Do you think he can see the lights around you?

M: (Positively) *Oh, yes! He can see. He can see. I don't think there's anything he can't see.*

D: He must be a very remarkable person.

M *He is. He came to us! As I said, his light has expanded to take in our light. We are now part of his light.*

D: What is he doing?

M: (In awe) *The children are glowing. The children are glowing. They...* (she was making sounds of awe and delight). *Alive... yes, the energy is... Oooh! My whole body is tingling. Oooh! The children... oh, the children* (chuckle). *They are being children. They are tugging at his sleeve and the edge of his gown, and asking him to kneel down — which he is doing. He understands the children. Yes, and the children respond to him. As if this man is a grown up result of what they have been being fed a spoonful at a time. It's as if 'Oooh!* **This** *is what we can become!* **This** *is why we're learning what we're learning! Look! This is what it's like when it's all grown up!'*

D: They can sense this?

M: *Yes. Oh, there's... we have been taken into his light. It's a most wonderful... unusual...* (Her voice was so filled with delight that she had difficulty completing sentences).

D: Feeling?

M: *Yes. The whole thing is as we are out of time and space. We are all in this sphere of white light* (deep sigh). *Well, he wants to know what the children have learned.*

D: Oh, he's talking to them?

M: *And 'What is your favorite game?' and 'What is your favorite song?' And 'Can you show me?' And... But the children are too excited to come together and...* (delightful laugh).

D: Did the crowd follow him?

M: *There are people, yes, down there. It's as if the children have transformed the crowd also. Now I don't sense the crowd so much as black, dense lumps, but more as a grouping of colors, many colors and textures and shapes. They are not distinct, but there is a crowd there. We are not on the same plane that they are on.*

D: Do you mean something happened when he came over to you?

M: *Yes, We have... we are suspended in this* (chuckle). *We are in our own world* (happy laugh). *It's very pleasant.*

D: Is he talking to you also, or just to the children?

M: *It's as if he understands who I am. And that it does not need to be spoken to. It's as if he is being an example for the children. That his presence here, the time that he has spent with them in this moment, will stay with them all of their lives. That is his main purpose for coming over, for the children to have this experience of energy and bonding and being lifted up in this white light. And being*

*suspended out of time and space. The children will
remember this **always**... even into other lifetimes. They
have had this contact.*

D: Did he talk to them, or do you think just being around
them was enough?

M: *He knelt down to them. He is on their level. He has his
arms around them. The children are excited and
communicative. He seems to be able to understand all of
them at the same time.* (Pause) *He looks up at me.* (An
intake of breath) *Oooh! He understands so much! Oooh!*
(She was almost overcome by emotion).

D: What is it?

M: (Almost crying, her voice was quivering:) *He
understands. He understands the pain in my head. He
understands the knowledge that I'm not being allowed to
share. Oooh! He loves me, for what I am able to do. It's as
if this is enough. To work with the children. To share what
I can with their young, developing minds will be enough. It
will be enough. Oooh! That man! I believe that he took
away the pain.*

D: Did he touch you?

M: *No. But it's gone.*

She was so immersed in her incredible experience that I felt
almost like an intruder.

D: Did he speak to you, or did he just communicate this to
you mentally?

M: *There was an understanding between our minds. He... he
has the same burden. He has so much knowledge and
understanding. And it's as if he's not being allowed to
share it either. That may have been the connection
between us that drew him over here* (deep sigh). *We have a
similar path. We have an understanding.*

D: Did he stop talking to the crowd while all this was happening?

M: *Yes. He had finished with what he had to share with them.
It was as if coming over to us was a very private act on his
part, and the crowd was not involved in it. They were
simply bystanders. They were there and they witnessed,
but they didn't participate. Nor do I think they understood
even what they witnessed. I wouldn't be surprised if we*

were invisible, too (laughing). *We were very, very high.*
D: What do you mean, very high?
M: *Oh, I mean... we were very expanded in the light. It's... we just glowed.*
D: The other people probably didn't even see anything out of the ordinary. What is he doing now?
M: (Softly) *I have a calmness now that is hard to stir myself out of.*
D: Is he still there?
M: *I believe he is still here. I seem to... have left my body. And I need to come back into my body.*
D: Yes, for the children. You can't leave them there.
M: *Oh we're all safe. It's just... until I come back into my body, I'm not much good at what* **we're** *doing* (deep sigh).

She was taking deep breaths, apparently in an effort to reassociate herself.

M: *It was a healing. As if he took into himself that which was so painful for me. He really has released me. And I know that's why I'm having a hard time coming back.*
D: Maybe your head won't bother you so much any more.
M: (Softly) *It* **is** *gone. The* **pain** *is gone. I believe that's what he does. I believe he has that ability. I believe that he could surround one of those lumps of coal and they would become a diamond* (soft laugh). *I believe he has that kind of understanding and... level. He's at a level that I've never known. I'm not even sure I understood that there was this level. He is still with us. We are still in the sphere of white light, but we have been suspended. We are out of time. The children are out of time with us.*
D: I imagine it's a very strange feeling, but it's not unpleasant. (I wanted to be sure she was comfortable).
M: *Oh, no. Who would want to leave* **this**? *No, this is a very exalted level.*
D: I wonder why the other people don't feel it whenever he speaks to them.
M: *I believe they have not opened their bodies and minds to receive this. It's almost as if he has given us a gift as an acknowledgment of our attainment. That he has helped us to advance on our path, simply by coming over and* **being** *with us. By taking us into his light and into his vibration.*

> *It is as if he has given us a gift. We will all be **different*** *when this is over.*

D: Then he didn't have to touch you, or talk to you?

M: *No. What he did was acknowledge the children on their level, so they understood how important they are. Each of them individually is a very worthy soul, with their own special gifts and their own special tasks. And by kneeling down with them, and touching them and allowing them to touch him, they had a complete validation of their individual spirits. And as he stood and became one with me, they witnessed the transcendence. This allowed them to transcend and know their spirits outside their bodies. They now have this truth of the reality of the spirit that dwells within.* (This was all spoken softly and in great awe.)

D: And no one can ever take that away from them. Maybe it was easier for the children because they were more open.

M: *Yes, they are still new spirits in these young bodies. They haven't been* (chuckle) **densified**.

D: That's a good word.

M: *They are still light. Well, I'm sure this cannot go on forever. We are... we are returning to our everyday state.*

D: Which is quite different.

M: *Yes. And so he must go. He blesses us as he walks down the stairs. He says that he doesn't often have this opportunity. And that it was a special treat for him as well as us. As if we were special. We were as much a gift to him as he to us.*

D: That's very good. You did have a part to play, to help him also.

M: *Yes.* (She addressed the children:) *Well, now, children. That was an experience, wasn't it?*

D: What do they say?

Ignoring me, she addressed the children, and then began to reflect on the experience.

M: *We can attain to that. As he was, so can we be. We have our small understandings that prepare us for larger understandings. And whether we are able to touch as many people as we want in this lifetime, we know that our souls have made enormous progress in this one moment.*

We have achieved a gift. It's as if... oh! The enormity of the gift is overwhelming. Oh! It's as if we have just been catapulted years and years and years ahead of our present place. That he was able to collapse time, It is as if we are many lifetimes more advanced now than we were just a moment ago. The children are now very subdued with me. They realize that we are now different. (Deep sigh:) *It's also time for us to readjust into our bodies and minds. It's dusk. The parents are coming to get their children.*

D: I wonder what they will tell their parents, or if they will?

M: *I don't know. The children have different degrees of understanding with their parents.*

D: This seems to be a once-in-a-lifetime experience.

M: *Yes. It seems that way to me, too. That this was... an enormous gift.*

D: Who was that man? Do you know?

M: *He never spoke his name. I never asked. But he was of the light. He **was** as a Son of God. He had a higher understanding than any of us have reached on the earth at this time. It's as if he was the embodiment of all the mysteries that I have been taught. That he was how it looked when you did them. He was as a finished product. What he shared with us was... he **elevated** us to a different dimension. And by doing so let us experience what **we** are capable of doing also.* (Sigh) *And so....*

D: You said he was as the Son of God. Aren't we all considered to be the sons of God?

M: *Yes. He was just so much **closer** in his abilities. You know the lumps of coal that I mentioned earlier? They have a **long** path before they become that kind of light. The children and I are not lumps of coal, but nor are we at that level of light that he is. And **all** of us are returning to our light that emanates from God. This man, that he would walk the earth and be at that level is... I don't... I can't grasp it... he's a very special person.*

D: I don't think there are many around like that, are there?

M: *No. I've never met anybody like that. He has a mission. It's as if, as he left us he was returning to the path that he had set for himself to walk. And that this side-path to us... was just that. It wasn't the main path that he was walking. But it certainly was a gift for all of us that he would take this detour. It was as if the children and I fed him as well as him feeding us.* (Suddenly back to reality:) *And so,* (sigh) *the last of the children are leaving. It's time for me to light the candles. I will have much to reflect upon in my bed this night.*

D: Yes, you will. And I really thank you for sharing the experience with me. When I come again, will you speak to me of more things like this, and share your experiences with me?

M: *I cannot believe there will be more experiences like this.*

D: Even if they aren't like that. Will you share your knowledge with me?

M: *Yes, of course.* (Emotionally:) *I will share my* **life** *with you.*

D: I would be honored if you would.

M: *I need to be by myself now.*

D: I can understand that. I think it is important that you be by yourself now to reflect upon what has happened. And I do thank you and I want to come again at another time.

M: *Thank you.*

D: Alright. Let's leave that scene. Drift away from that scene, and let Abigail go to rest and reflect upon what she has experienced.

I then brought Mary back to the full conscious waking state. This experience was so profound it is impossible to convey the extreme emotion exhibited on the tape. Her voice was soft and caressing as velvet as she related the experience. She was totally in awe and swept up in it. I was deeply moved while listening to her and tried to absorb the wonder of it by osmosis. I often felt like an intruder by asking my questions. When I brought her forward and awakened her, she was still caught within the spell of the experience. She seemed to want to hold on to it as long as she could, knowing full well that it would soon evaporate. Although she was awake she lay quietly on the bed going over all the details in her mind. It was a total all-encompassing event of incredible beauty and she didn't want to let it go.

I turned the tape recorder back on, and the following was part of the conversation after awakening:

M: *I can remember being in my cell where I slept, with my eyes wide open. I don't know if it was still the charge of light energy around me, or trying to understand what had happened. But there was no sleep for me that night.*

I began speaking louder and moving around the room trying to break the spell she had created for herself.

D: Yes, that was quite an experience, wasn't it?

M: (She still wouldn't release it:) *We were... it was almost as if we were removed from the earth. It was almost as if we were caught up in this sphere of light. We were out of time and space. I can't help but think that we became invisible.*

D: I don't imagine anybody watching knew what was going on. They probably didn't see anything unusual.

M: *Maybe not. I don't know how that works.*

D: You said all those people were like lumps of coal. They probably didn't understand anyway. They probably would have just seen a man playing with the children.

M: *I don't know. Maybe that was an experience for them also. I think he was able to demonstrate that to the crowds, even though we were in our very own environment. The crowd* **had** *to be able to discern the change in our physical bodies, because there* **was** *a change in our physical bodies. We expanded. The light expanded our bodies. They* **had** *to have been able to... maybe it was a demonstration. That this man was saying, 'This is what is possible. See these children that are pure and new and unafraid. See what they can become. And see this woman who is full of trust and faith. See how she can be transformed. This is also what you can do.' I believe they saw a change of some kind.*

D: Yes, it's hard to tell how **much** they might have seen. Well, it was very beautiful. I think it's time to come back to the land of the living now. But it's wonderful that you can remember how it felt. You'll be able to keep that as a gift. Most people don't remember when they wake up.

M: *Well, there was an enormous release. My whole body was unburdened. I don't know where it went, but he was able to take it away. I don't know how he did it. But because he understood about the binding of my mind, it was as if I was able to release it. Because somebody understood.*

D: Do you think you'll be able to use this experience in your present life?

M: *I believe that this memory was a gift to me. And as I travel*
     further down my path in this lifetime, that I will be able to
     draw on it. Remember how I said that the children, as they
     grew older, whether they realized it or not, would have
     these patterns in their life? That is what has been given to
     me here. Whether it stays in my conscious mind or not, it
     can become a part of this lifetime now. And as I need it, I
     will be able to use it.

D: That's very good.

Normally the subject does not retain vivid memories of the
session when they are in a deep enough state to totally identify
with the other personality. But in this case I was to discover that
the subconscious had a valid purpose for allowing her to remember. The memory would not impair her present life, instead
it was to cause important changes that would greatly improve it.

Mary thought there would be no need for further sessions.
She had received enough to ponder on for several months. As
winter descended upon our Arkansas mountains we each returned to our normal routines.

About a month later we met again at a party, and Mary came
to me, threw her arms around me, and told me I had changed
her entire life. She said the regression experience had had a
very profound effect upon her. It had opened up a whole new
world for her. As we sat in a secluded corner she confided to
me that she had been married three times and divorced three
times. She always seemed to be looking for something that she
couldn't find. Her husbands were not bad people, they were just
human, yet she found fault with each of them. Now she realized
that she had experienced a profound and unworldly love for this
man in her past life, and she had been trying to recapture it ever
since. But she was unconsciously searching for it in mortal men
and it could never be found there, because such profound and
unselfish love was not of this earth. No human male could
possibly measure up to that. She had tried to find this incredible
emotion in all of her husbands, and because they were human it
wasn't there. In disappointment she kept searching instead of
settling for the lesser mortal love of a human man. She had not
consciously understood this search and need for perfection and
perfect love.

Mary said that since the regression her entire life had been turned around. A whole new world had opened up, and it was wonderful. For the first time in her life she had allowed herself to become involved with a man in the normal way, and it was a totally new experience. She knew now that she could have a relationship and let the man be human, faults and all. She felt as though she had been released from a terrible burden. Her unreasonably high expectations of what human love should be had been put in their proper place. She understood that such incredible love was real and she had experienced it. But she also understood that she would not find it again while she was alive, because it was not of this earth.

I wished to explore the life of Abigail again, but this was not to be. Mary became very busy with a successful business and a newfound love interest in her life. When I saw her from time to time she seemed to be happy and at peace with her life, but she felt no further need for regression. She believed she had found the solution to her most immediate problem, and that is the most important part of my work. My desire is to help people adjust so they can live in the most effective manner in their present lifetime, without problems and patterns from other lifetimes bleeding into it and interfering.

I was never able to find out what happened to Abigail. Apparently she was committed to service in the Temple and had to remain there. But I like to think that her life became easier after her encounter with Jesus. She said he had eased the pain in her mind, and showed her that her work with the children was important and would be enough, even if she never transferred the great knowledge she had been given. Maybe she devised increasingly clever ways to impart these teachings to the children, without the knowledge of the priests.

Certainly as the children grew older they would not have forgotten her kindness. Maybe they returned for further teachings. Maybe she found a special student. Whatever became of her in that lifetime, I feel Abigail's life was blessed by this encounter. I feel my life was also blessed by her allowing me to relive it with her. I too was able to feel the incredible love through her words. Abigail imparted more knowledge than she will ever realize by sending this information forward to our time period. Thank you, Abigail, you truly are a devoted, caring, and wonderful teacher.

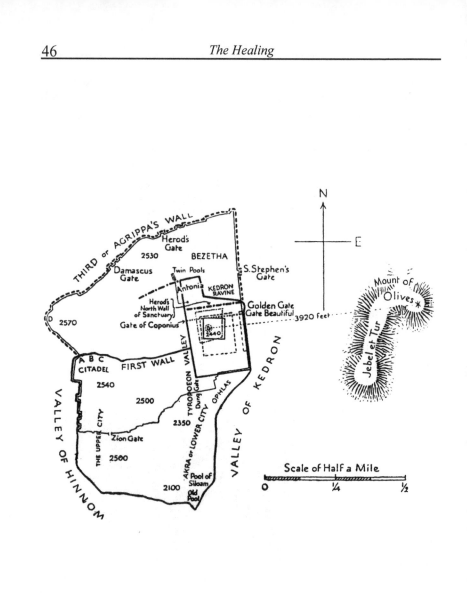

Herod's Jerusalem

A model of Herod's Temple from the South-east

Chapter Four

The Temple and Old Jerusalem

The material in this book was obtained in 1986 and 1987 through hypnotic regression into the subjects' past lives. It lay undisturbed in my files until my publisher suggested in 1993 that I write the sequel *to Jesus and the Essenes.* I knew at that time I would have to do the necessary research to confirm or deny the historic references and implications in the narrative. This is a necessary, and in my case, enjoyable part of my work.

The careful regressionist working in this field does not do any type of research until the sessions are finished. It has been suggested that if the hypnotist or the subject have any knowledge of the historical period or the material, it could possibly be transmitted unconsciously by ESP (Extrasensory Perception)— which I consider an important phenomenon in itself, if it could be proven. I have had subjects give indications that they are aware of things going on in the room, which they could not normally see or hear. They often answer a question before I have asked it, as though they are picking it up from my mind. I know I am not unconsciously supplying the answers, and they are not changing the story to fit what I am imagining, because I may have a picture in my mind of what is going to occur next, and it is often totally wrong. They seem to be telling the events from their own unique point of view, and I can do nothing to influence this. I have performed tests many times to prove, to my own satisfaction, that undue influence is not occurring. But if neither I or the subject have any prior knowledge of the material, historical period, or area, then the answers must be coming from somewhere else besides our own subconscious. For these reasons regressionists are advised to do no research until the case is completed.

In the last stages of preparing this manuscript I decided it was time to delve into the old dusty volumes in the university library where I do my research. If I cannot find what I want, they have a very reliable interlibrary loan system that can locate any book in the United States. Their computer finds the book, normally in other college libraries, and it is sent to me. This is the part of my work that greatly appeals to me. I love to search through old books, doing hours of reading to locate one significant detail. It is like finding a diamond in a pile of sand, and the search gives tremendous satisfaction.

Some of the information I found may be common knowledge to Jewish people who are interested in the history of their homeland, but it was certainly not known to me as a Protestant American. I will include it here in order to paint a picture of the area as it existed during the time of Christ. The proper surroundings are important for any narrative.

Millions of tourists travel to the Holy Land every year expecting to visit the same places where Jesus lived, taught and died. I found that this is impossible because these places no longer exist. Even those hoping to walk the same earth that Jesus walked will find it to be impossible, because the very terrain has changed so much.

Today Jerusalem is a sacred city for three of the most important religions of the world: the Jewish, Christian and Muslim. For the first two it is recognized as *the* Holy City, and for the third, second only to Mecca and Medina. Probably for this reason more than any other, Jerusalem has maintained its continued existence — and for this reason, it can never die so long as humankind continues to have any religious belief at all.

For this book I was concentrating on finding details about the old Temple of Jerusalem, and about Jerusalem itself. I wanted to see if Abigail's description of the Temple could be verified. What I discovered amazed me. It is known that many ancient cities have disappeared and all traces of them have been buried by the sands of time. These are often found through diligent research and uncovered bit by bit by the archaeologist's shovel. However, I have always assumed that if a city has remained in the same location for thousands of years, that remnants of the old civilization would be preserved. I have seen ruins in England dating back many centuries. Rome still has ruins of the

Colosseum and other ancient structures. Thus I thought the same thing would be true of Jerusalem. It has been the center of so much religious attention down through the ages, I assumed that some of these ancient sites would be preserved.

I found that this is not true. Amazingly, I discovered that absolutely nothing from the time of Christ has survived. No sites were walled off and kept for posterity, because at the time the events were occurring there was no hint of the importance and influence they would have on the world centuries later. It may come as a shock to find that the majority of the sites shown to devout pilgrims have no foundation in fact. The Christian churches in Israel were built on *supposed* sites of his birth and death, and so on, and are *presumed* to be the correct places, but are not necessarily authentic. The greater part of the holy places shown in Jerusalem have been gradually selected during the course of many centuries for the benefit of Christian pilgrims, and some of the sites have been moved about, or grouped together, for greater convenience.

Over 3,000 years, the Jerusalem area was conquered and occupied by many different civilizations and cultures. The city has passed through a constant series of alteration, demolition and reconstruction. Material used in one age has been used again and again, sometimes being scattered in the process to different sites. Works which may have served one purpose, have been altered and reconstructed, so as to show hardly any trace of their original use. The area of the Holy Land and the sacred spots have changed so much that few locations can be identified with certainty. Even the exact spot of the old Biblical city of Bethlehem has not yet been ascertained. It was without doubt a smaller city than that of today. Scholars are now saying that, even though the population swelled during the census, there were probably no more than fifteen boy babies born there during that crucial time. This made is easier for Herod to keep track of them, and the consensus is that there was probably not the massive slaughter of babies that is depicted in the movies.

The present city of Jerusalem is built largely to the northwest of the ancient city. Nevertheless it is possible to recover a fairly accurate picture of the city of Jesus' time. From the Mount of Olives one could look directly across the Kedron Valley at the Holy City. In the time of Christ Jerusalem sat high on a hill, and the Temple Mount was surrounded on three sides by massive walls. It gave the impression of a mighty fortress sitting in an inaccessible position, and indeed had stood the test of time against countless enemy attacks. Sheer cliffs dropped on the east, west and south sides down into steep valleys (the Kedron Valley and the Hinnom Valley), and served as natural defense ramparts. In Christ's day the city was separated by a ravine, the Tyropoeon Valley, and divided into two clearly defined parts. This deep valley was crossed by a large stone viaduct or causeway, supported by huge arches.

Jerusalem has been destroyed and rebuilt so repeatedly that city overlies city. In some places the modern streets are nearly one hundred feet above the level of the old town, buried under debris that has accumulated over much of the ancient city. The Tyropoeon Valley today is largely filled up and remains only as a shallow depression called el-Wad. Thus, even the topography of the land around the Holy City has changed considerably since the time of Christ. The area originally was several distinct hills and valleys, and has now been transformed into a nearly level plateau. The valleys surrounding Jerusalem have been filled up with the accumulation of ages.

The broader and higher hill on the western side of the Tyropoeon Valley was the site of the Upper City, which the ancient historian Josephus called the Upper Market. It may be assumed that this part of the city was originally a market center. The lower eastern hill, which sloped down from the Temple area, was called Acra and was the site of the Lower City. The Temple area itself was the "third hill". North of the Temple was the "fourth hill", where the growing city was spreading out. This last and newest part was called, according to Josephus, Bezetha (probably meaning "House of Olives") and also New Town. This area was not yet walled in the time of Christ. Jerusalem at that time was much more a hill city than it is today, and the houses were built on the steep slopes. The narrow streets frequently took the form of steps and were therefore impassable for carts and riders.

The Jews liked to consider Jerusalem as the center of the world, and it could indeed be called the hub of the ancient world. The many different nationalities of Palestine, and the great influx of foreigners to Jerusalem, caused a great variety of human types to be seen, and a variety of tongues to be heard in her streets. Greek, Hebrew and Aramaic were the main languages. Many of the nationalities had their own quarter in Jerusalem, and especially their own synagogues and temples.

Some of the tremendous walls that surrounded the Temple Mount originally were along sheer precipices that dropped up to three hundred feet to the valley floor below. Excavations seem to confirm Josephus' claim that in the days of King Solomon the tremendous western wall was exposed to view throughout its whole height, measuring eighty four feet from the bedrock to the level of the pavement of the Outer Court, and above this the cloister's wall rose high above the Court. This description was thought for years to be an exaggeration by Josephus.

Another wondrously constructed stone bridge once spanned the deep ravine of the Kedron Valley on the eastern side of the Temple, and united that section to the Mount of Olives. This was described as a causeway constructed of arches standing upon arches, the upper arches springing from the crowns of the lower ones. In those times there were enormous substructures, which were built to obtain a level surface between the irregular natural hills. On the far side (the Mount of Olives) there was formerly a twisting stairway, leading down into the valley and then up steeply to the east gate of the Temple area. There was a spacious promenade or terrace fifty feet broad in front of the Golden Gate entrance in ancient times. Jesus is said to have entered Jerusalem by this direction from the Mount of Olives on Palm Sunday. Terraced gardens also beautified the slopes from the Kedron bed up to the high terrace by the Temple wall.

Josephus tells us that in the time of Jesus Jerusalem was completely honeycombed with underground galleries and subterranean passages, used not so much for drainage or burial, as for purposes of war. Every ancient stronghold had its secret passage for escape in time of danger. When the Romans invaded and destroyed Jerusalem in 70AD, they found that so many fugitives had taken refuge in the subterranean chambers that it was necessary to burrow underground in search of the enemy. A hundred fights took place in the very bowels of the earth. There were so many dead bodies in these tunnels that a poisonous stench came up from every trap and vent, and the air of the city was unfit to breathe. To prevent the spread of disease, the Romans stopped up the traps and vents, and walled up the openings into the secret passages. These old sections were in time forgotten and many were lost.

There have been several temples located on the Temple Mount. In our time the Dome of the Rock, a Muslim holy place (mosque), sits on the site of the former temples. The site is now called Haram esh-Sherif, meaning "sacred enclosure", and is indeed sacred to Christians, Jews and Muslims. It has been three thousand years since King David selected Jerusalem as the most suitable place for the capital of the kingdom of Israel. King Solomon (c973-c933BC) built the first temple at Jerusalem from plans drawn up by his father David. Solomon's Temple occupied the site where the present Dome of the Rock now stands, although the modern sanctuary doubtless covers a greater area than the Solomon structure. It has been conjectured that the Holy Rock, underneath the ornate Muslim dome, is the natural summit of the hill and was the site of the Temple building itself. This rock may well have served as a natural altar from primeval times. The Temple and Palace of Solomon were enclosed within a wall and separated from the main part of the city itself. Nothing now remains above ground of these structures, though considerable sections have been discovered underground. We only have the records of ancient historians to help us imagine the reconstruction of the site.

The history of Jerusalem is a long and turbulent one of takeover by many different countries, and centuries of construction, followed by total destruction, and then rebuilding again. More thorough excavation is required to have sufficient data on the validity of any existing theory, and formulate an accurate reconstruction of the ground plan of the Jewish Temples. Such data does exist, but at present it lies buried under a vast accumulation of rubbish, the debris of many centuries, and sits beneath streets and houses, so it cannot be easily excavated. Subsequent rebuildings have caused great destruction in the areas of the ancient city that have so far been excavated.

The Rabbis have a tradition that the original copy of the Law is buried within the sacred enclosure of the Haram (the area surrounding the Dome of the Rock). And it is commonly believed that the Ark of the Covenant, which suddenly disappeared and was never seen after the destruction of Solomon's Temple by the King of Babylon, was concealed and still lies hidden in some cavern beneath the Temple Hill.

Somewhere within the walls of the Holy City there is the royal sepulcher of the Kings of Judah (as reported in the Bible). In that royal vault rests the dust of David, and round about him on either side would be Solomon and the successive princes of the House of David, who were buried in the same sepulcher. Archaeologists believe that when the Royal Tombs are found they will be a complex of chambers and not a series of individual chambers. Historians claim that King Herod the Great knew where the burial chamber was and removed some of the treasures buried with the kings. He wanted to conduct a more diligent search, but two of his guards were slain by a mysterious flame that burst out from the sepulcher. This frightened Herod and he abandoned the tombs. They supposedly were never bothered again, and their location has disappeared.

Jerusalem was captured by King Nebuchadnezzar of Babylon in 598 BC, and again after a rebellion, in 587BC. On the latter occasion in particular, the city suffered terrible devastation. The Babylonians completely destroyed the city of Jerusalem — the Temple and the walls were broken down, and the inhabitants were exiled. No major reconstruction was done until after 538BC, when Jewish exiles were allowed to return from Babylon after fifty years in captivity. At that time the city of Jerusalem was slowly and painfully rebuilt. Nehemiah authorized the rebuilding of the walls and the Temple on the same site as the Temple of Solomon, but on a smaller and poorer scale. This Temple stood for about five centuries, but some of the masonry suffered from decay and neglect. These accounts of this Temple are recorded in the Old Testament.

The Romans entered the picture many centuries later when the Hasmonean ruler's sons Hyrcannus and Aristobulus quarreled over the throne. This opened the way for the fall of the land to the power of the Romans. Eventually Rome made Herod the king of Judaea, a position he occupied from 40 to 4BC. Herod the Great was an enthusiastic builder, and it was under his rule that the city of Jerusalem attained the appearance it had at the beginning of the Christian era. Jerusalem was turned into a far stronger city than it had been since the time of David.

Herod was very unpopular among his Jewish subjects. As he grew older he sought to put himself into favor with the people. He was a man of considerable taste in the art of masonry, and knowing the deep veneration the Jews had for their national sanctuary, he conceived the idea of rectifying some of the bad feelings and rendering himself popular by rebuilding the Temple. It also provided work for a very large number of men, and reduced the threat of revolution. The king's offer to rebuild was at first received with doubt and suspicion, but Herod fulfilled his promise. Yes, this was the same King Herod who forever secured his evil reputation by killing babies in his search for the infant Jesus.

He repaired the walls and built three powerful towers into the old city wall. Adjoining the three towers was the palace of Herod. When Judaea was later ruled by the Roman procurators, this huge building became their residence and seat of government while they were in Jerusalem. At the northwest corner of the Temple area he built an elegant fortress for the soldiers, called Antonia (named after Mark Antony), which was connected with the Temple porticoes by two stairways or bridges, so they could have access to the Temple area immediately if there was trouble. From the fortress' vantage point a constant watch could be kept over the city, the suburbs and the Sanctuary.

Herod's most important architectural enterprise was the re-building of the Temple itself. Although he claimed to be doing the work as a public benefactor, it was probably actually prompted by vanity. The work began in 20-19BC, and the rebuilding of the sanctuary itself was completed in a year and a half. The main part of the new building was finished in about eight years, but the work of embellishment and the erection of the outer courts was continued throughout the whole period of Christ's life. The existence of Herod's stately Temple was very brief. Within forty years Christ's prediction that "there shall not be left one stone upon another, that shall not be thrown down" *(Mark* 13:2) came true when the Roman invaders destroyed the remarkable edifice.

All remains of the Great Temple of Jerusalem have disap-peared. When the Romans assaulted Jerusalem in 70AD the huge and wonderful Temple was burned and completely razed. Except for Herod's palace, which was retained for administrative purposes, the whole of Jerusalem was swept out of existence. Many of the walls were dug up even to their foundations, and the stones thrown into the ravines. The Romans wanted to give the appearance that Jerusalem was no longer inhabited, that it no longer existed. It was complete, total demolition, and all the inhabitants were either murdered or removed during one of the worst bloodbaths in history. To further desolate the entire area the Romans deforested the immediate neighborhood of the city, then the land within a radius of over 11 miles. They thus turned a heavily-forested, vineyarded, and gardened area into utter wilderness. Palestine never recovered its former appearance. This was the time that Qumran, the Essene community at the Dead Sea, was also destroyed. The fortress of Masada was taken, but not before hundreds of people committed suicide there, following a long siege by the Romans.

Since that time scholars and archaeologists have tried to determine exactly what Herod's Temple looked like, and where it was located on the Temple Mount. The only remains above ground are the sections of the massive walls that have survived. The walls themselves were marvels of engineering and technology, described by Josephus as "the most prodigious work that was ever heard of by man". The bases were placed on the solid rock bed up to one hundred feet below the present surface. Massive rocks weighing several tons apiece were discovered. These rocks were placed so closely together that a piece of paper could not be inserted between them, and no mortar was used. Remains of this typical Herodian masonry can still be seen in the Wailing Wall on the western side of the Temple area.

Above ground this wall appears to have been reconstructed, because the stones are not fitted together as carefully now as they were formerly. The nine lowest courses of stone consist of huge blocks, as was characteristic of Herodian masonry, the largest one being sixteen feet long and thirteen feet wide. Above this are fifteen courses of smaller stones. There are many indications it is a reconstruction from old material. It is difficult to believe that the original builders, who took such pains to obtain magnificent blocks of stone with finely-chiseled faces, should have placed these other stones in such a haphazard fashion. The Jews have been coming to the Wailing Wall since Biblical times to lament the destruction of the Temple.

There are many theories about the appearance of the Temple in Jesus' day, but few facts. Some of the ancient historians — Josephus is the most notable — have left descriptions and references in their work. The Temple was built of hard limestone which was quarried from huge caverns deep beneath the northern part of Jerusalem. This type of rock could be polished to a high sheen to give the resemblance of marble. The Temple area was blessed with an inexhaustible water supply, which came from a natural spring. There was a wonderful system of underground reservoirs interconnected by pipes and conduits. Some of this system still exists in the underground chambers beneath the present city.

According to Josephus, the walls of the outer Temple court were lined with porticoes, and the basilica on the south was especially notable, having at least one hundred and sixty two columns. Each pillar was a single block of the purest white marble, and was so large that three men could just reach around it with their arms extended. These four rows of pillars included three spaces for walking in the middle of these cloisters. The roofs were adorned with beautiful sculptures in cedar, and the front was made of polished stone. This was the first thing encountered after entering the gate through the massive outer wall. From there the open court was paved with all manner of stones. There seemed to be no special reason for this large pillared basilica, unless it was designed to protect large crowds of people against sun and rain, or to attract trade. There was a lot of business conducted on the Temple Mount, connected with the selling of animals and birds for sacrifice, and money changers.

Beyond the basilica was a large outer court commonly known as the Court of the Gentiles. Although in the ancient Temple of Solomon only Jews were admitted within the walls, Herod felt that he must appropriate some part of the Sanctuary for the use of strangers of all nations. This was because there were many Egyptians, Greeks, Romans and members of other nations resident in Jerusalem. Thus a large outer court was constructed, open to all who wished to walk and converse in this cloister, which was therefore called the Court of the Gentiles. Adjoining this was the Court of the Israelites, into which no Gentile was permitted to enter on any pretense whatever. Josephus states that these two courts were separated by a low wall or balustrade about four and a half feet high, with thirteen entrances or openings. On the top of this partition small square stone pillars were placed at intervals, each bearing an inscription in Greek that no stranger should pass the wall, and threatening death to any transgressor.

The Temple was a huge complex composed of various courts, one leading into the other until the inner court and Holy of Holies was reached. The people were allowed to enter each court according to their worthiness and cleanliness. This was all defined by the Law, or Mosaic set of rules. On the east side of the Temple Mount was the Women's Court. This was approached by entering through a portico consisting of tall pillars (called the Hall of Solomon), and then climbing a series of terraced steps, because this area was sloped at more of an angle than the rest of the Temple Mount. The steps led from one area to the next, progressing from the Women's Court up to the main Temple area. Ancient historians say the flight of steps was probably broken by two wide landings, with a third wide step at the top of the flight. Possibly these steps extended the whole length of the Porch.

Jewish men could go inside this area into the Women's Court. However, most women could not progress further because they were considered to be unclean most of the time, due to their menstrual periods and the after-effects of childbirth. Certain men were also not allowed to go further into the inner courts, if they had any type of infection or disease, or if they had recently come in contact with a dead body. There were many rules regarding the cleanliness of the people, and most Jews fell within some of these categories at one time or another.

Beyond the Women's Court were several more into which only certain people were allowed, until the final holy chamber was reached. This east entrance to the Women's Court was distinguished by folding doors of Corinthian brass. Josephus says that occasionally public gatherings took place in front of them. They were so massive that it needed the combined strength of twenty men to open and close them every day, because it was unlawful to leave any of the Temple doors open. There were nine other gates and doors to these inner courts that were completely overlaid with massive plates of silver and gold, as well as their doorposts and lintels. But the huge brass gate far exceeded them in size and value.

In the Priests' Court, and directly in front of the Temple edifice proper was the altar upon which sacrifices and burnt offerings were made. There was a series of rings in the floor where the sacrificial animals were tethered to await their doom. The area also contained eight marble tables on which the carcasses were skinned, washed and prepared for the altar. The blood of the victims drained off through holes in the floor, and the whole area around the altar resembled a butcher's slaughterhouse. Here the burning of the incense, and the blessing of the people, was done in front of those who were qualified to enter this Temple area.

Not only the whole facade of the Temple house, but the wall and entrance between the porch and the sanctuary, was covered with gold plates. The sanctuary itself stood within this inmost court and was approached by a flight of twelve steps. It was built of white stones, each of which Josephus assigns the enormous size of approximately thirty five by twelve by eighteen feet. It is said that it was in its day the largest religious sanctuary in the world. In front its height and its breadth were equal, each being one hundred cubits (nearly one hundred and fifty feet), according to Josephus. It was covered all over with gold plates, with a concave golden mirror hanging above the entrance. This mirror reflected the rays of the rising sun with fiery splendor.

Inside the sanctuary were the customary divisions of the Holy Place and the Holy of Holies. In the Holy Place there was an altar, a solid gold seven-branched candlestick, and a light that was never extinguished. The walls of the Holy of Holies were overlaid with gold, but contained absolutely nothing, because no images were allowed. The high priest was the only human being allowed to enter this most sacred chamber, and then only on certain special days. The Holy of Holies is believed to have been situated over the present Sacred Rock inside the Dome of the Rock.

Only the entrance to this sacred section was visible to the people. This was covered by a rich six-colored curtain which moved in the wind. This curtain hid the gilded interior and its contents from all laymen. This is the curtain that was rent in two from the top to the bottom at the time of Christ's crucifixion.

As seen from the Mount of Olives, the Temple was directly in the foreground, where the Dome now rises over the sacred Rock. Surrounded by sumptuous colonnades, its courts rose one within the other, each higher than the last to the inner Sanctuary itself, whose marble and golden facade gleamed and glittered.

Herod's purpose apparently was that the Temple should be visible from a long distance, and that it should dominate its surroundings. The building material of snow-white limestone,

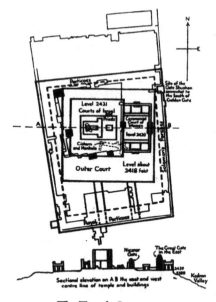

The Temple Sanctuary

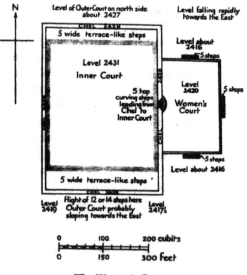

The Women's Court

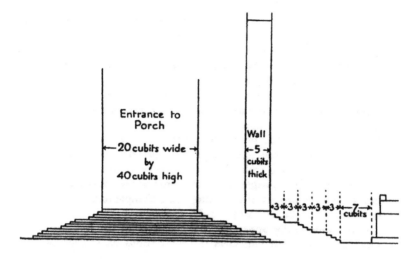

The twelve steps approach to the Temple Porch

and the square front entirely covered with gold, were meant to divert the attention from all the rest of the city. It was therefore quite natural to swear by the gold of the Temple.

All of this extensive building required huge sums of money. Herod levied taxes excessively and ruthlessly, and was always thinking of new ways to subsidize his many projects. The people were also taxed harshly by the Romans to finance even greater expenditures abroad, which brought no benefits to Herod's subjects. The people found these burdens oppressive. There were bitter outcries against the squandering of money that had been wrung from the people's very life-blood. Herod thought that if the people could see some of the money going into the visible project of rebuilding their Temple to their God, that they would be, at least partially, appeased.

One cannot fully appreciate the character of the Jerusalem sanctuary unless one considers the conceptions of "sacredness" and the ritual preparations which those who desired to "appear before the Lord" had to undergo. Some were encouraged to extend the purity-ordinances into everyday life, so as to not arouse God's wrath. The views of Jesus were different. He did not attach the importance to the various stages of holiness in the sanctuary as his pious contemporaries did. He felt they were preoccupied by focusing on the ritual and ceremony, rather than what these stood for. They had forgotten the individual person and his needs.

I believe the area where Abigail was conducting her children's classes was on this east side of the building. There were several other flights of stairs leading from the Court of the Gentiles into the Women's Court, but the terraced group of stairs seems to fit the description of dancing on broad landings. It would also be sensible that the priests had delegated Abigail to the Women's Court, as befitting the status they had placed her in. She was again being kept in her "proper place". Near this outer area was a chamber for storing musical instruments, which also fits with her description of the dances.

There were pillars at the eastern end of the portico, which could be the place where Jesus was speaking to the gathered crowd of people. The huge pillared area to the south (the basilica) at the entrance to the Temple Mount was too far away for Abigail to see and hear him clearly. Historians seem to agree that Jesus and his disciples taught in the area at the east side of the Temple. It would make sense because there he could speak to anyone, regardless of their degree of cleanliness. Also he could be heard by Jew and Gentile alike, because this area beyond the barrier was open for all.

If my assumptions are correct, then Jesus would have been speaking at the lower edge of the Women's Court under the pillared portico, while Abigail played with the children on the terraced steps leading to the inner courts. If he turned and saw her, he would have climbed the stairs towards her, while the crowd watched from below. I think the historians' findings and interpretations of Josephus have identified this as the only area where this could have occurred. And most remarkable of all, the stairs, the pillars and other details are all there. These are verifying facts not readily accessible to anyone who had not done the exhaustive research.

In the following chapters I will insert items relating to this research at their appropriate places.

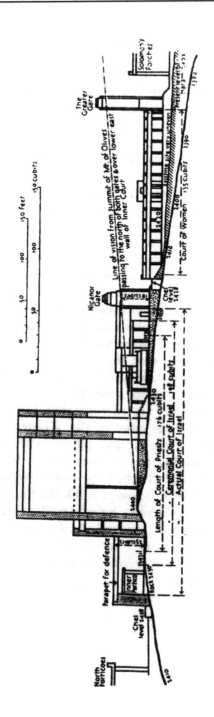

A sectional elevation of Herod's Temple

Chapter Five

Introduction to Jesus' Niece

The next surprise connection with Jesus occurred spontaneously in 1987, a year after my work with Mary. I was still deeply involved with the translation of the Nostradamus quatrains (for the three-volume *Conversations with Nostradamus),* and I had now become a UFO investigator. I was called upon to perform hypnosis in suspected abduction cases in Arkansas (see my book *Keepers of the Garden).* My time was divided between many projects, plus past-life therapy.

Anna was a very gentle, soft-spoken Jewish woman in her late thirties, although her appearance belied her age. She seemed to possess an eternal youthfulness, and gave the impression of hiding an impish teenager just beneath the surface. She was raised in the Reformed Jewish Temple, and she and her family did not know Hebrew. Anna and her husband had decided to escape from the crowded and noisy conditions of Los Angeles, where she had been born and raised. They chose to live a quieter lifestyle in our Arkansas hills, and built a bed-and-breakfast establishment on the outskirts of a nearby tourist town. I had known her for several years, and had worked with her as a subject on many projects. She had proven to be an excellent subject and I had conditioned her to go quickly and easily into deep trance. I can truthfully say that Anna is one of those rare individuals who are incapable of deception. She is the most trustworthy person I have ever met.

At the time of this incident Anna was not having any problems, and we were not working on anything particular. She had been experiencing recurrent scenes that flashed into her mind. These scenes appeared similar to Israel or that part of the world. They were just simple street scenes and glimpses of people dressed in typical garb for the area. They were not disturbing, but she thought maybe her subconscious mind was trying to tell her she had lived a lifetime in that country. She wanted to explore the possibility. We intended to see if we could find any information about it during this first session.

When she had made herself comfortable on the bed, I used her keyword and began the session.

D: You said you've been seeing some scenes lately that you think might be connected with a past life. We're going to see if we can find out anything about that, and if there's anything there that you need to know about. You thought it might be in Jerusalem, but we don't know for sure. So if the scenes that have been coming into your mind have importance and if they have validity, I'd like us to go and explore them and see if there's something there that you need to know. I will count to three and on the count of three you will be there. 1... 2... 3... we have gone to that time you have been visualizing. What do you see? What are you doing?

She entered the scene at an unusual point. She spoke with a childish voice, and was experiencing such emotion that she seemed on the verge of crying.

A: *I'm... I'm a woman child. I am not yet thirteen years old. My name is Naomi* (pronounced: 'Niome'). *And I'm not very happy* (close to tears). *Oh, it's hard to talk about.*
D: Did something happen to make you feel this way? (She was sobbing, so I pacified her). You can talk to me.
A: *I wish that I was a man child. Then I could be free to do what I believe I'm supposed to do. And I know that* (she broke down). *This is hard.*

Anna already knew me and had a working rapport with me, but I was dealing here with another entity. I had to obtain Naomi's trust so she would feel comfortable talking with me.

D: I understand. Sometimes you need someone to talk to. You can always talk to me about it.

A: *I'm supposed to be spreading the teachings, because I understand them so well from my heart. And he looked at me and he told me I couldn't, because I was a woman and it wouldn't be understood. And...* (sobbing) *I love him so much.*

D: Who are you talking about? Who told you this?

A: *This* was... (sobs) *this was the Nazarene.*

The only person I had ever heard called this name was Jesus. This was a surprise. I would have to ask questions carefully to determine if this was whom she was talking about.

D: Do you know the Nazarene?

A: *Yes* (sobs). *And I wanted to leave my parents' house and walk with him, because I* **know,** *I know I can do all those things.* (Her voice was full of sorrow and emotion). *And I'm not afraid.*

She began to cry, the tears trickling down her cheeks and soaking into the pillow.

A: *I could cut my hair and walk in boy's robes. And I don't think they would know the difference. But I believe, I* **truly** *believe that I'm supposed to walk by him, and help him and take care of him. I believe he needs me. And I believe that if I had been born a man child, then I could have done this. But there is nothing else for me to do. I don't want to do anything else.*

D: I understand.

A: *And they say my father is his half-brother* (sniffle). *And if that is so I think I should be allowed to do this.*

This was a great surprise. I assumed she was speaking of Jesus, but did he have a half-brother? In *Jesus and the Essenes* it was mentioned that he had several brothers and sisters, but we did not come in contact with them in that book. Although I was confused, I had to think of ways to ask questions that would not be leading.

D: Who is your father?
A: *My father is the forge-master. He works with metal. He's the village metalworker. He makes locks and various things with the different metals he forms.*
D: You said he is half-brother to this other man?
A: *That's what I was told. I don't know if that's why they want to keep me from him or not.*
D: What is your father's name?
A: *Joseph.*

Another surprise. I had found that in that culture the oldest son was often named after the father.

D: How long have you known this other man?
A: *I've **always** known him. He's **always** been there. He comes to the house to see my father. I guess they have business together, but he has another business in town. I have heard him speak and it was as if he was speaking my words. I know he's **leaving**, too.*
D: Where is he going?
A: *He's taking a group and he's going on a journey, a pilgrimage to spread the teachings. And I know that's my place. But my father doesn't feel this way. My father feels fear, and I don't. My mother is a very quiet woman. She doesn't say anything about it.*
D: What is the city or the town that you live in? Does it have a name?
A: *Jerusalem. They say...*

She spoke three words that were apparently Hebrew, a language which Anna has no conscious knowledge of. They were difficult for me to transcribe phonetically, so I later asked a man who was fluent in Hebrew if he could understand them from the tape recording. He said, "Of course", and gave me the spelling: *Yerushalaym shel sahav.* Naomi continued:

A: *And now I know what that means. I never really knew what that meant.*
D: What does it mean?

A: *It means 'Jerusalem of Gold'.*

The Jewish man said that this translation is absolutely correct. He then explained why Jerusalem was called that. The older houses are made of a local honey-colored limestone, which gives all the town a golden glow when struck by the sun. This sounded like a plausible explanation, until I did my research into old Jerusalem. All of the buildings in the modern city were built after the time of Christ, so this would not fit unless the houses were made from the same type of material two thousand years ago. That is a possibility, but my research disclosed a much more logical explanation for calling the city "Jerusalem of Gold".

I found that the main Temple buildings had been built of local white limestone polished to such a sheen that it resembled marble. The front of the buildings had been gilded with a plating of gold, and several of the huge doors leading to the inner court or sanctuary were plated with gold and silver. All of this gave the impression of a glistening Temple, and must have made a very impressive sight. The Temple was described as so beautiful that it was spoken of throughout the ancient world. Apparently the people called the city "Jerusalem of Gold".

A: *I have always liked the sound when I heard it, but I never knew what it really meant. And it meant what he's spreading. It meant that golden glow that I see coming from his heart area. It's that golden glow from loving and caring and kindness, from there not being fear or cruelty. So it means that kind of gold. The gold of* **being***. It doesn't mean the gold of the metal.* **That's** *what I didn't understand. So it means that he has made Jerusalem of gold, because of what he's trying to teach. And I guess, now that I understand it, I just want to live it. I want to be of help. I want to walk with him. For I know I have that same loving energy, and I could be of help. And I don't need to be married or taken care of, or be a mother. I know I could walk with him and learn to heal and ease other people's pain. And that's all I want.*

D: You said you knew some of his teachings. Have you studied with him or what?

A: (Laugh) *No, that's not allowed. I have heard him talk to my father, when they thought I was sleeping. I have also disguised myself and sneaked out to where he was holding a meeting. And I've listened when I've sneaked out and done this.*

D: Does he have a large group of people? You said he was taking a group with him.

A: *No, not very large, because most people have been doing the teachings in private, in small groups. But he knows now that he is supposed to send his messages out. This group is small because not many of us are brave enough to walk the path of truth and love. It is hard to find people who are not afraid to heal and be of service. So right now the group isn't very big, from what I know.*

D: Do you know him by any other name besides the Nazarene?

A: *They call him Jesus, but I think I like the way the 'Nazarene' sounds better. Maybe it's because I hear my father and him talking. The Nazarene.*

D: I was wondering if that was what your father called him.

A: *Oh, sometimes. But usually, when he comes over, when they talk of the business, the carpentry and the metal, he calls him Jesus. Sometimes he calls him brother. They use 'brother' a lot.*

D: But you said you heard they are half-brothers? Does that mean they have the same mother or the same father? What do you know about that?

A: *I don't know if I understand it all. They have never really talked about it, or they would not talk in front of me. But I think... I think the father is the same, because my father has the **name** of his father. But I don't understand a lot. They've never told me.*

D: Have you ever seen your grandmother and grandfather? (I was thinking of Joseph and Mary).

A: *The ones of my mother more than the ones of my father. There are things they don't talk about. We don't see them very often. They are far away. That's what they tell me.*

D: Then the one you see most of that family is the Nazarene, when he comes? Do you have any brothers and sisters?

A: *I have a brother. And he is far away. He went to study.*

D: What kind of study?

A: *He went to be learned. He went to study with teachers and raboni, to learn various Laws and Teachings. To be a learned man.*

I could not find the word "raboni" in the dictionary, so I asked the Jewish man about it. He said it is one of the formal respectful ways of addressing a rabbi.

D: Did he have to go a long way to do this?
A: _Yes. He had to go to another larger town to do this._
D: I thought Jerusalem was large.
A: _Jerusalem is large. But I think for his studies he could not stay in Jerusalem._

I have already explained that education meant the study of the Law exclusively. Any other type of learning would have to be obtained elsewhere. The idea occurred to me that her brother might have gone to study with the _Essenes,_ since Jesus was quite familiar with them.

D: Then you don't really know where he went? You never heard anyone say?
A: _He didn't give me the name. No, I don't know the name. But there are many things that they don't let me know. I think out of fear, or they think they are protecting me._
D: But this brother is older than you, is that correct?
A: _Yes. This brother is ten years above me. I do not know... he might be involved in things that are secretive. So they tell me what they tell me. It's like he is another father_ (laughing). _My mother has my brother and I as children, but she has other children she cares for. And she does all those things that are expected of women to do. But she takes care of orphan children or children that need to be watched over._
D: Can you tell me what the Nazarene looks like? What his physical appearance is?
A: _He is... when I look up at him, I'm not sure. Let me see first. For a man he's about the height of my father, which I guess you say is average. He seems very... he's strong in the arms and the shoulders. He's not a very big man, but he has strength. And... his eyes, his eyes are wonderful. His eyes are blue. And he has brown hair and... hair on his chin and above his mouth. And he's tan from the sun. I would say he's fairly dark-skinned._
D: But you said his eyes are wonderful?

A: *Yes. I never thought that blue eyes were kind and loving,
but his are. I am used to dark eyes. But his eyes are just so
kind, so loving* (sigh).

In *Jesus and the Essenes* I quoted from *The Archko Volume,*
a little-known book written by Drs. McIntoch and Twyman,
printed in 1887. These men had discovered written reports in
the Vatican Library dealing with Christ. One of these contained
a description of Jesus that remarkably coincides with the
descriptions given by the various subjects. After *Jesus and the
Essenes* was printed I came across another such letter which
contained a similar description. This startling document was
also discovered in the Vatican Library. It was supposedly
written to the Roman Senate at the time of Christ by Publius
Lentulus, then Roman proconsul in Judaea, a predecessor and
friend of Pontius Pilate. The following is his description of
Jesus:

"This is a man of noble and well-proportioned stature, with a
face full of kindness and firmness, so that the beholders both
love him and fear him. His hair is the color of wine (probably
tawny) and golden at the root — straight and without luster —
but from the level of the ears curling and glossy, and divided
down the center after the fashion of the Nazarenes.

"His forehead is even and smooth. His face without blemish
and enhanced by a tempered bloom; his countenance ingenuous
and kind; his beard is full, of the same color as his hair, and
forked in form; his eyes blue and extremely brilliant.

"In reproof and rebuke he is formidable; in exhortation and
teaching gentle and amiable of tongue. None have seen him to
laugh, but many, of the contrary, to weep. His person is tall; his
hands beautiful and straight. In speaking he is deliberate and
grave and little given to loquacity; in beauty surpassing most
men."

This was taken from the article "What Did Christ Really
Look Like", by Jack Anderson, which appeared in *Parade
Magazine,* April 18, 1965.

D: You said he has been coming to your house for as long as
you can remember?

A: *Yes. I have always known him. I have always seen him*

there. When I was very little I just thought they did business together, but I think he was trying to heal a family problem.

D: It would be natural, if they were brothers, that he would come from time to time to see him. I'm very interested in this man. He sounds very unusual.

A: *Well, I just... I know I went to him the other day and I told him I want to walk with him. (Sadly again:) And he told me that, being a woman child, it would be too difficult. People would not understand. And I told him I could cut my hair off and wear robes of men, and they wouldn't know. And he said that I would walk with him, but the time was not now. And I don't have any wish to do anything else. I am not my mother's child. I am not made to do the things she does. I am just in this woman's body.*

D: Maybe he meant that you would have to wait a while. If he said the time was not now, he didn't really say no. Maybe he will let you go with him later.

A: *I hope so. But I can be of service anyway, and try and remember what I have heard him say. And help my mother with those children that need such care.*

D: You said you sneaked out one time, and listened to him speak. Was it only one time?

A: *Well, there haven't been many opportunities, because I do not like to dishonor my parents. But I was so **pulled** by my voices to go listen to him. So I was there a few times. I would hear, in our little part of town, where meetings were held, or overhear people talk to my father. They were held in various places. People had secret parts of their homes, or underground spaces in the town area. And he would hold a meeting and teach a way of life that is **right** and should exist for all.*

During excavation the archaeologists discovered that the underneath portion of Jerusalem is riddled with secret passages and underground chambers dating back even before the time of Christ. Some of the houses could have had secret entrances leading to underground meeting rooms.

D: Can you remember some of the things he said?

A: *Well, when I think about it, I can see the glow of the golden light around his heart area. And I remember most*

*that he said just to love and care for one another as you
would have them do to you. I guess that's what I remember
most. His wisdom is strong, and yet it is not* **brutal***. So
he's teaching that you do not have to inflict pain on
another in order to have understanding.*

D: Why does he have to meet in hidden places?

A: *Because there's a group in the governing powers that are
beginning to think he might have an influence on more
people than they thought. I don't think they believed in him
or took him seriously in the beginning. And I think they
are worried now because the poor and the helpless, the
ones who have faith and believe, are turning towards him
more and more. So there is a change in the feeling from
the governing bodies. They are becoming harsh. They are
becoming afraid of his power of truth. They are a wasteful
bunch of people. They take and take and have rooms full of
wealth, and care not what happens to the sick and the
poor. So the meetings are held in secret.*

D: I wonder why they would be afraid of one person.

A: *They weren't in the beginning. But I think some in the
governing bodies have heard him. They know he speaks a
truth which they are feeling in themselves. And within
themselves they are torn, because they cannot feel
allegiance to the other body. So great conflict is being
created, I am afraid.*

During this time Israel was burdened under the heavy yoke
of occupation by the Romans. They had had many of their freedoms taken away, and were being excessively taxed, to the
extent that many of the Jewish people felt like slaves in their
own country. They were looking for a redeemer, a Messiah, a
savior, to come and deliver them from the situation. They
desperately wanted the lifestyle returned that they had enjoyed
before the Roman occupation. But there was also great fear,
because the Roman army was strong.

Many secret groups were forming, advocating the overthrow
of the government by violence. One of the most notable was the
Zealots, of which Judas Iscariot has been identified as a
member. They wanted war and were looking for a leader strong
enough to organize their movement. Many of these groups,
some violent and some peaceful, thought they had found such a
leader in Jesus, because he was speaking of things they had

never heard before.

The priests did not like him because he preached a philosophy that was different from what they were teaching. Thus he was watched carefully by both groups. The Romans were especially diligent because they saw he was gaining followers, and they knew the civil unrest only needed a strong leader to organize a revolt. The wide dispersion of the Jews had caused Jerusalem to become a center of considerable magnitude in the Roman Empire. Whatever took place there, took place on the world's stage. Thus any action by a subversive like Jesus was carefully watched and reported to Rome.

D: You say he has a group that goes with him most places? Do you know any of the people in that group?

A: *There are a few men I have seen. They don't really let it get out in the public very much. But it seemed they are men of his age. There seems to be a bond, a following. They believe in the same things and are working for the good of the whole. So there are a handful that I always see around him.*

D: I was wondering if you might know any of their names. You know I won't tell, I'm just curious.

A: (Pause) *There seems to be a man called John* (said as a question). *And this man... I've seen John a lot. But these other men, I don't think I know their names.*

D: I thought you might have heard him or your father call them by name. What does John look like? You said he's about the same age?

A: *Yes. He looks similar, except he has the dark eyes of many of the people around this area. And he's not as kind-looking. He's a bit huskier, too.*

D: You said a while ago something about your 'voices' telling you to do something? What did you mean by that?

A: *Well, I don't like to dishonor my parents or go against their wishes, but sometimes I hear things. The voices coming into my head tell me these things are all right, because you do them for the right reasons. You do them not with dishonor. You do them because you are honoring your faith, your God. The voices are so strong that I know it's alright to disguise myself and sneak out of the house.*

D: And this is what you mean. You hear them inside your head? Do you have any certain religion, or do you know what I mean?

A: *They don't teach the woman child very much, at least not for my family. But they are of the Judaic belief. I think, too, the Nazarene is of this belief. Yet he is walking a different path, because there is much unkindness in the Laws. So I think that is why families are being torn. People are having trouble understanding or knowing their own beliefs now.*

This was part of the conflict Jesus had with the priests in the Temple. He did not agree with their interpretation of the Law, the Mosaic rules that had been set down for the Jews to follow. He thought they were unfair and interpreted too strictly. In *Jesus and the Essenes* it was obvious that in his study of the Laws he found other meanings. His outspoken remarks caused friction, so he had turned away from the Temple and resorted to telling people in secret about his versions of religion. As his popularity grew, so did the opposition of the priests, who thought he was trying to undermine their authority.

D: Does your family go somewhere to worship?

A: *They do. They go to the Temple.*

D: Have you ever been to the Temple yourself?

A: *Yes. But women go in a different way and sit in a different place from men. And I don't...* (sigh) *I don't feel very loved in there. I feel closer to God elsewhere.*

D: Can you tell me what the outside of the Temple looks like? Is it a big building or a small one?

I wanted to see if Naomi's description of the Temple matched Abigail's.

A: *This one... I think there are many around.*

D: In Jerusalem?

A: *Yes. This one is not the biggest. This is of stone or stone structure.*

D: Is there a larger one in the city?

A: *There's a larger one.*

D: Have you ever seen that building?

A: *I've seen it. It's very big. It scares me. It makes me feel cold.* (Laughing:) *I like our smaller one.*

D: Why? Because it's too big?

A: *Yes, I think it's just too big.*

D: Well, what does that one look like from the outside?

A: *Oh. It has many of the light-colored stones. And then I see large doors, and some pillars on the outside. There's... it's very high-ceilinged inside.*

D: Does it have many pillars around the outside?

A: *In the front, seems to be... eight in the front.*

D: Does it have pillars anywhere else but in the front?

A: *Inside, I see some inside.*

D: Does it have steps going up to the doors?

A: *Yes. They're long... long stones ...steps.*

Naomi's description coincides very well with Abigail's version and with the historical research.

D: But you said you don't like to go there because it's...

A: (Interrupting:) *Too big. It makes me feel lonely.*

D: Yes, sometimes things can be too big, and then it sets you apart from what they're trying to teach you. But the women are not really taught lessons?

A: *No. Not where I have grown up. They don't teach the women. The men are educated. The raboni will teach the men, but he doesn't teach the women. It seems to be a tradition right now. I am not pleased with it.*

D: It seems strange that they wouldn't want to teach you, because you do want to learn.

A: *I have learned. I have learned anyway. I have listened and I have learned. And I have had friends that have taught me.*

D: Well, the group that follows the Nazarene, are there any women in that group, or is it just men?

A: *I see women. But I don't know if they are with the group all the time, or if they are there because they are wives and sisters. But he seems to be going with the men on the journey.*

D: I was thinking that if there were other women in the group, maybe you might be allowed to go later.

A: *Maybe. There's a Jeremiah. Jeremiah's coming to my mind. I'm not sure why. I think he is one of the men that go with him.*

D: Is Jeremiah the same age as the others?

A: *No. He seems a little younger.*
D: This country that you live in, does it have a ruler? You were talking about a governing body a while ago?
A: *They call him king. King? I guess they call him king, and then he has a ruling body, I guess.*
D: Have you ever heard them talk about the king?
A: *My father has. They think he's an unjust king. They... it's like I told you, they have rooms and rooms, storehouses of wealth, and there are too many poor people out there.*
D: Have you heard of anything he has done? Did your father ever talk about any certain thing?
A: *Well, he... they talk about people they call 'slaves'. They talk of cruel punishment. They talk of people who are taken away and never heard from. And there isn't any reason behind it.*
D: Do they think the king is responsible for these things?
A: *Yes. And I don't quite understand it all. I don't know everything there is to know. They don't tell me these things. You see, my mother is a very good, quiet woman. She's just what she's supposed to be. So she doesn't discuss any of this, or have an opinion she will talk out loud about.*
D: Maybe that's what is expected of her. Do you have a large house where you live?
A: *No, it's small. My father has his work space, and then connected to it is our living space. And outside there is a cooking oven. So it's small, but it's nice. It's comfortable.*
D: What does it look like on the inside? The living space?
A: *It is one room when you walk in. That is where we have meals. We have a table and furniture. Then there is another little room where my parents have their bedroom. And there is a little cellar door. And then I have a little alcove area for my space.*
D: What does your place look like? What do you sleep on?
A: *It is straw that has been tied together to give it shape and thickness. It has been put on a little platform of wood. And then it has been covered over with cloth and skins.*
D: Is it comfortable?
A: *Yes. It's just very comfortable.*
D: Is that all you have in your little space?
A: *I have that and a candle. And then just little personal things, but that's all. And my robes are folded up in one*

corner.
D: What kind of food do you eat?
A: *We eat grains and fruits. And there is fish. There are what they call 'dates' and other soft-type fruits from bushes.*
D: Do you ever eat meat, besides fish?
A: *Rarely. Once in a while we have lamb. I don't know... beef? Beef?* (as though it was an unknown word)
D: What is that?
A: *Beef is rare. We have that very little.*
D: Do you have any kinds of vegetables, or do you know what I mean?
A: *Yes. Vegetables we call... squash and... there are green type of vegetables.*
D: Well, it sounds like you have many different things to eat. What do you drink?
A: *I drink goat's milk and water. And there's a different kind of drink for my father.*
D: What is it?
A: *I think he drinks a brew. I don't know exactly what it is though. And then they also have wine. We make breads in our oven outside.*
D: So you don't go hungry. That's very good. Well, would it be alright if I come again and speak to you some time?
A: *Yes, I would like that. You made me feel better* (relieved sigh).
D: Alright then. And you can always talk to me when I come and tell me things that bother you, because I don't tell anyone else. It's always good to have a friend to talk to.

As I brought Anna back to full consciousness, I wondered how she would react when I told her what she had just talked about. She had some vague memories of the session. I left the tape recorder on as she reported these.

D: You said they had different names for the food? And you could hear other languages coming in? Is that what you mean?
A: *Yes. It's hard to explain. When you'd say 'vegetables' or fruit', I could picture it but I couldn't give it a name. There were also some things I have never seen in this life'. So I think sometimes when you ask me questions I'm trying to filter the answers through so much that's going on*

around me.

D: You could hear other languages? Were they in the background or what?

A: *Sometimes. But I didn't understand the words.*

D: Are those few things all that you remember?

A: *I remember the house. And I think I remember...* (laugh) *I remember saying 'the Nazarene'.*

D: Apparently that referred to Jesus. Do you know very much about him?

A: *Because I am Jewish I haven't really thought about Jesus much in the past. Never, in fact. In my background he wasn't even acknowledged. In the household I grew up in, I would ask mom and dad about Jesus, and they'd just brush it off. Jews that I knew when I grew up acted like he didn't exist. So it wasn't until I was in my thirties that I really started facing that issue. I always thought there was a conflict. I couldn't understand why they wouldn't talk about him. And yet the little bit I was learning about him, he seemed like such a good teacher. That's why I never had any frame of reference for him.*

D: So you have no reason to... for instance, a Christian might say, 'Oh, I wish I had lived in the time of Jesus'. You would have no reason to feel that way.

A: *No, because we didn't even talk about him. He didn't exist as far as my family and the people I knew.*

D: If I told you that you had known Christ in that life, what would you say?

A: *I'd say...* (laugh) *I don't think I can respond to this* (laugh).

D: What would you say if I told you he was your uncle?

A: (A stunned expression) *I didn't know Jesus was an... I just... I find it really confusing. I find it almost comical. This is absurd. I am Jewish. To have such a story coming from me has to be the worst possible choice.*

D: It's hard to believe, in other words.

A: *Well, right now I'm uncomfortable with it. Ever since I was a child, because of my parents... nobody ever told me about Jesus.*

D: But they didn't play it down either?

A: *No, my parents really wouldn't have known how to talk about it. They always had pat answers. There wasn't a whole lot of communication. As a child I just learned what to ask and what not to ask. I learned at a really young age that there were certain things you didn't ask about. And they just said, 'There are Jewish people and there are non-Jewish people. We believe in God'. They used to tell me, 'They've got Jesus. And to us, Moses, who gave us the Ten Commandments, was like our Jesus'. These were the kind of things that my parents would tell me. Now I'm trying to remember my childhood. When I was little, I could barely tolerate going to Temple and Sunday School. I thought it was all a bunch of malarkey. As a little kid when I was learning Jewish history, I was appalled at how cruel the Jews were. It was so clear to me how much control they had over your lives and how cruel the Temple was. I have had those feelings about Judaism since I was a child. But I heard from all the other little kids about Jesus. And I grew up being so offended by him. I was appalled that this whole religion was created around this one man, so I never felt anything good about Jesus. It was always very offensive to me. And then when I got older and started to question it, it got even worse. I didn't even understand who he was or what he was. I just felt it was too strange to comprehend, that people would have formed a religion around a man. Religion is supposed to be about God. It wasn't until we were living here that I started listening to what some people had to say. And all of a sudden things became clear to me. This has all just happened within the past five years. So it was as if I had to get away and maybe into this kind of environment to let things clarify in the right way. As if 'This is the truth, this is what I needed to know'. Maybe that's why I could never swallow any of what I heard, because he was a human being. But also because... maybe a part of me inside wants to believe it. Especially because over this past six months, for some reason I've had such strong feelings and I don't know where they are coming from. I knew there was something significant for me to check out in that area of the world, and that regression was the way to find the answer.*

D: But this wouldn't be something you would want to invent if you were going to fantasize a past life.

A: *That would be the last thing I would ever think of.*

This seemed to be a remarkable breakthrough, and I definitely wanted to follow up on it and obtain her story of the life of Christ, as she had contact with him. The fact that she is Jewish gives this story a great deal of validity. I asked her if she had ever read about Jesus in the Bible. She said she only had the Old Testament part and was not even very familiar with that. They were not required to read it in their religion. When she tried to read it on her own she said it was too difficult, too taxing. So I asked her not to read the New Testament. She replied that there wasn't much chance of that because she did not even own a copy of it. As far as she was concerned she knew absolutely nothing about his life, and none of the events that are so common to Christians, or the stories that are drummed into us from childhood. This was all foreign territory to her and she would have nothing in her subconscious to draw on. She would also have no conscious or subconscious reason for fantasizing. The whole idea seemed absurd to her. This could be a perfect chance to obtain a story that would stand up to the criticism of the skeptics.

The idea of Joseph having an older son bothered me, and I wondered how people would react to that. However, I knew that Joseph was a great deal older than Mary. This was established in *Jesus and the Essenes*. What occurred in his younger years? Perhaps he was more human than the Church has led us to believe. Perhaps he also had frailties common to us all. Whatever stains there were on Jesus' family tree, it apparently did not bother him. He had been friendly with his older halfbrother for years. I wondered what other unknown details we would uncover as we proceeded with Naomi's story.

Chapter Six

The Departure

I wanted to explore the Jerusalem life further, to see how much association Anna's alter ego Naomi had with Jesus, and how much information she would be able to give me. I used her keyword and counted Anna back to the time that Naomi lived in Jerusalem.

D: I want you to go to an important day in your life when Naomi lived in Jerusalem, and tell me what is happening. I will count to three and we will be there. 1... 2... 3... it's an important day in your life. What is happening? What do you see?

A: *I see the same scene I have been through before. And I know now what I must do with my life. I want my parents not to feel I have been disobedient, but I know my destiny is to walk with him and teach. And I am willing to wear the robes of men and disguise myself, for I am not meant to do things like my mother, or be obedient as she was. The only thing I see for me in this life is teaching his words and his ways of living.*

D: How old are you at this time?

A: *I think I am thirteen. I have aged about a year, because in that year I **tried**, I really tried to be a good daughter, and do as they wished. But it is not in my heart. I love them,* *but my life is not worth living if I have to stay here and marry and live that sort of lifestyle.*

D: As every other girl would have to do? Have you discussed this with your mother and father?

A: *My father isn't that patient, and he called it foolishness. I have stopped talking. And my mother understands, but 'it's not the life for a woman', she said. So I have become quiet, and I have just prayed. I have talked to the Nazarene when he's been here, but there aren't any more choices.*

D: Does your father also think what his brother is doing is foolishness?

A: *Not at all. He believes in all the words and what he is trying to do. He's just not used to a woman or a girl following in those footsteps. If I were a man child I believe there wouldn't be a problem. They might fear for my safety, but they would let me go with their love and blessing.*

D: They are just trying to protect you. They have your welfare at heart, even if it's not what you really want to do. They're thinking of the best thing for you.

A: *I know. And I tried, I tried for almost a year now. And I did things that they wished. I helped my mother with the children. And I can no longer do this. I feel old beyond my years. I feel, for me, marriage is foolish. There is no reason for me to marry. The only things I love are the truths I want to help spread to people. And I love... I guess if I were ever to love any man, it would be the Nazarene. But I know this is never possible. So that part of me has to learn to love in a different way from the way a woman would love.*

D: Isn't this going against the tradition as to what a woman should do in your time? Maybe that's why it's upsetting your parents.

A: *But I know I'm meant to be a teacher and a counselor. And this is all that is in my heart. I know it is the only right thing for me to do. I only hope they are willing to understand and realize that there was no choice. There is only one path.*

D: Have you thought that when you get out there, it may be harder than you think?

A: *I have no fear of that. I have no fear of death or hardship.*

I find things are very simple. I find that there are only very few reasons for me to be living at all. And there is nothing in me that is capable of being what my parents think I should be. Even though it is from their heart and for my own well-being.

D: You said you talked to the Nazarene about this. How does he feel about it?

A: *A year ago when I talked to him, he gently placed his hands on my face and said I was a woman child and that I could not walk with him now. But I would walk with him at another time.*

D: Yes, I remember that.

A: *And I know, too, that he was merely talking for my parents to hear. But I looked in his eyes and he knew better. He was doing it out of love and protection. And I told him then that I could wear men's robes and cut my hair and no one would be wiser. I know he will not turn me away. He knows I have stopped talking about certain things and have gone quiet. And he knows why, although I haven't told him. He knows I will walk with him and he will accept me, because he knows it comes from my heart and from God.*

D: He might have thought you would change your mind because you are a child.

A: *But he saw in this past year that I tried to be an obedient daughter and do as my parents wished. He knows I have done the best I could, and I tried. But it would be wrong for me to marry and have children, because it would be without the truest love in my heart. I cannot make a happy home with what is in my heart.*

D: You would be only doing it out of duty more than anything else. But he probably thought you would change your mind. At your age people usually don't know what they want to do. Well, what **are** you going to do?

A: *I am waiting to hear when he will be leaving again.* (Firmly:) *And I will go.*

D: Is he there in Jerusalem at this time?

A: *He is expected within a few days.*

D: Do you know where he has been?

A: *I think he has been out at his family home. And there have been problems there. But he is continuing his teachings and meetings and traveling to towns.*

D: With his group of people?

A: *A small group.*

D: Where is his family home? Do you know what town that is?

A: *It's away... It's the Nazareth area, but from where I am it's a few days of walking, I believe. I have never been there.*

D: But his home is not right in Nazareth. Do you know what members of his family are there?

A: *Their brother... I think their brother is at home. And there have been some difficulties. I'm not exactly sure. They don't talk that much in front of me, or if they know I'm nearby.*

D: Well, because you were talking about family, I wondered if he had ever married. (This was a trick question).

A: *Oh, no, he would never marry. He is married to God and his beliefs. And he feels that is his reason for being alive. He could not be as faithful or as dedicated to a woman and family.*

D: Then the ones that live in that family home are mostly his brothers?

A: *Yes. His parents' home. He has brothers in that area.*

D: I was surprised that he was having family problems. I thought that things would go smoothly.

I was trying to find out what was going on without being intrusive or obvious.

A: *I think his brothers have some kind of a problem.*

D: You said before that your father didn't see his parents very often either. Was that because of a family problem, too?

A: *I think, from what I remember hearing, that his father had trouble acknowledging him. Because the woman he calls mother... did not remain with his father.*

D: You said before that he and the Nazarene were half-brothers.

A: *I don't know if I can explain it. I think his mother was not able to marry his father. And there was a problem. And I know she was ill. I don't think I know all the information.*

D: In other words, you think that the Nazarene and your father, did not have the same mother? Do you know which one is the older? Your father or the Nazarene?

A: *My father is older than the Nazarene.*

D: And this is one reason he doesn't have contact with his family?

A: *Yes. I think there is pain, a great deal of pain and confusion and embarrassment. But it happened a long time ago.*

D: Apparently it doesn't bother the Nazarene at all, does it?

A: *I think he must know the whole truth. My father and he have worked together, and their beliefs are similar.*

D: I was curious because it sounds as if they are keeping secrets. Do you think the problem is with the other brothers? You said they were also having family problems, or do you think that's something else?

A: *Yes. I think there's some kind of jealousy, some kind of problem.*

D: Someday you may know the whole story, and you'll be able to tell me. I can understand why they wouldn't want to talk in front of you. They don't want the children, I guess, to know the family problems. Well, in your country, is it the custom to name the oldest son after the father?

A: *I think the custom has been to name children in memory of somebody, so they would live on through them.*

D: You said your father has the name of his father.

A: *Right. And I think my grandmother named him Joseph just to keep the love and memory of the father alive, because she knew that she could not be with him.*

D: But he did marry the mother of Jesus and the other children?

A: *Yes. I don't really know if it was an illness she had that had something to do with it.*

D: But you said you don't see your grandparents. Is that because they're so far away, or because of this problem with his birth?

A: *I was told it was too far away, but I'm sure my father is part of the problem.*

D: I'm just asking questions because I'm curious. If you go with the Nazarene, what do you expect to do? Do you know any of your duties?

A: *I will keep learning. I hope to be able to assist him in any way he wishes. I am not afraid to be with the ill or the poor or people who are in desperate need. I want to be able to give and learn what he does to help and heal. And live God's laws.*

D: Do you think he can teach you these things?

A: *I think he can.*

D: Does he know how to heal people? Have you ever seen him do anything like that?

A: *Yes. I once saw — I wasn't supposed to be there. He had a meeting in our village at night. I remember sneaking out, and I was hiding. And there was a child... a mother brought her child who was ill. I am not sure what was wrong with this child, but I saw him take it and hold it. He laid the child on his lap, and placed his hands on it. And the child stopped crying. The fever left, and the child was well* (this was spoken almost in awe).

D: Do you know how he was able to do that?

A: *I don't know. I think... he knows ways of living God's laws. And through love and caring he can make a difference, if it's supposed to be.*

D: This is not the normal way people cure illnesses in your time period, is it?

A: *No. We have physicians and they attend to the sick ones usually. But I know what I saw that night was a miracle. I don't know what was wrong with this child. But it was crying and very red and very sweaty, and in much pain. And it went from that to being calm and a normal color. I hope to learn how to help in this way.*

D: It would be a very wonderful thing if you could learn to do something like that. Have you heard of him doing any other healing like that?

A: *I have heard of him healing a crippled man. And I hear talk, but I don't really know. I have to wait and ask him.*

D: What kind of talk?

A: *Oh... how he can give people sight or heal limbs so people can walk or use them again.*

D: But you don't know if it's true or not?

A: *I hope it's true. I know what I saw. But some things, no matter how much you believe in God, it is really hard to believe that a man can do them.*

D: Yes, a mortal man. He must be a very wonderful person if he can do these things.

A: *He's... different. You know, when you see him or talk with him, or when he touches you, he's different from anyone else you have ever met. And that's why he could never... be with anyone else. Because this is what his life is meant to be, and only this. And I know just out of love and what I have heard from my prayers and voices and from God, that this is the way I am supposed to live. I am supposed to live singly and devote myself to these things I believe in.*

D: If that's what you really believe in, I suppose it's right to do whatever you wish.

A: *And I do not feel like a child.*

D: Have you heard any stories of other things he has done that have not been normal?

A: *Oh... I heard he went away and was educated differently from people in our schools, or in our temples. And he learned things from wise men in faraway countries. I think they probably taught him much about the healing, and how if your heart is pure and aligned with God, you are capable of changing physical beings and yourself. I think this might be part of the problem at home. I think maybe there might be some question within his family. But...*

D: What kind of question?

A: *Of things he can do. Things he was taught.*

D: Do they think this makes him different? Is that what you mean?

A: *Yes. And I don't know if they believe.*

D: Well, you know there are many other ways of educating besides your schools. They might have been able to teach him many wondrous things in other lands. But the other brothers were not allowed to do this?

A: *No, I don't think they had the desire. I think most of them wanted to live basic lives like most of the citizens.*

D: Then they shouldn't be jealous if they didn't want to have this kind of life.

A: *No. But I think there might be some doubts in the village, and it makes their lives more difficult. Or maybe they are embarrassed.*

D: Yes, they could be. Maybe that's what the problem is. Because these people have known him since he was a child, I suppose.

A: *Yes. And who else has been capable of doing these things?*

D: Do you think they might think he is faking or it is like magic of some sort?

A: *I think some of them do.*

D: They think he might be trying to fool people. I can see that would cause a problem if it's something that's so hard to believe.

A: (Sigh) *Well, I see him now.*

D: Is he coming?

A: *I see him... I picture him in my mind right now, and he's walking up the road. And I see this... energy about his head, a glimmering crown about his head.*

D: Have you ever seen that when he was present with you, or is it just in your mind right now?

A: *I have never seen it before.*

D: What do you think it means?

A: *I think it means 'truth'. I think it means to hold on and have faith. And that it's alright to walk with him.*

D: He sounds like a very wonderful person. But have you heard stories of anything else out-of-the-ordinary he has done, besides the healing?

A: *I have heard... yes, I remember my parents talking. There was someone else in the house. I guess they thought I was asleep. And they said, in an area that had suffered because there was no rain, and people were doubting him... he created rain. I heard them talk about that.* (Quietly, in awe:) *I forgot about that. This happens around here at times. We have some years where you get very little water.*

D: Well, that would be a form of a miracle, too, wouldn't it?

A: *Yes. But the main thing he wants to teach is God's laws to live by, and how to really love one another. That you can live in peace and without fear and jealousy. And that living with loving kindness is the true nature of man.*

D: But sometimes these things are difficult to teach to other people. It seems so simple, but some people don't want to listen.

A: *I know. That's why he has had arguments in the Temple. Because he found that many of their ways are very cruel and unloving. That's why he took to his path of walking and spreading the laws of God, and the ways men and women should live.*

D: These problems he had with the Temple, was that before he began going out and spreading the word?

A: *Yes. This caused him to leave.*

D: Do you know what happened?

A: *It was more than one thing. It was the fact, too, that they did not want to do much to help those in need, the poor and the suffering. It was the fact that they had little understanding and mercy when it came to looking at the problems of people, and passing judgment. It was a number of things.*

D: You mean they were judgmental?

A: *Very judgmental, and strict. And without cause.*

D: Was this the priests or the rabbis?

A: *Yes, the rabbis. There was only one way for everything. And it was unfair and unkind in many cases. The rabbis let their position and power distort their decision-making at times. They were the ones you go to to solve disputes and problems. And they felt that* **they** *became God, instead of* **listening** *to God and trying to be fair.*

D: Power can sometimes do that to people.

A: *Yes. So instead of trying to be of service and help dissolve the problems, they tend to create more, at times.*

D: So they are trying to go strictly by the Law, without having any mercy or any other interpretations? And this made Jesus angry or what?

A: *It made him very disappointed. He realized that what he was hearing in the Temple or through the rabbis was not what he felt God wished. He did not feel they were living the Commandments. He would question what they said, and ask why it could not be* **this** *way. And they were not used to being questioned.*

D: They were used to having their word as law.

A: *Right. And he would come up with a solution that would solve the problem quite well, showing justice* **and** *mercy and equality. And there were ways for the people who were the wrongdoers to make amends. So he would come up with solutions and challenge theirs, and this created many problems. I think it angered the rabbis because the Nazarene had more clarity and more fairness in his solutions. But Jesus could not deal with the hypocrisy and cruelty, because it is not God that is unloving and unmerciful, it is man. So he felt that his Temple was now the land, the earth was the floor, the sky was the ceiling. He would spread God's Laws and try to be a teacher.*

D: It sounds very wonderful. I can see why they would consider him a rebel, if he went against the teachings of his time. How did he find his group of followers? Or did they find him?

A: *There have always been those who felt the way he did, but were too afraid. So the meetings just started in various homes, and word-of-mouth. And people just followed.*

D: And after a while they wanted to stay with him? Is that what you mean?

A: *Yes. Because when you hear him speak you know there is truth. He speaks from his heart and from God.*

D: He does sound like a wonderful person. I can understand why you would want to follow him. You were talking earlier about your village, but I thought you lived in Jerusalem.

A: *Well, it is Jerusalem, but there are little sections.*

D: I'm trying to understand what you mean.

A: *There are areas of this city. This portion? They call it the East, and it was once called the East Gate. So I think these different portions got their names from various gates of the Temple. I guess these villages formed by people who were of the same beliefs living closer together. And I guess depending on wealth, too.*

D: Is there a wall surrounding the Temple, with gates? I'm thinking of a gate as usually being in a wall of some kind.

A: *Yes. This was originally the large Temple, and there was a wall around it and various entrances. So this was the East side. They have various names, but it's all the city of Jerusalem.*

Josephus said in his historical writings that the Tyropoeon Valley divided Jerusalem naturally into eastern and western parts. These were known as the Upper City and the Lower City. It sounded as though Naomi was saying she lived in the Lower City, which was located on the eastern side.

D: Are there any other large significant buildings besides the Temple?

A: *The Temple is the largest, most significant building. But there are other large buildings, the government offices, official offices, storage buildings, schools.*

D: It is a large city then. I've heard there might be other kinds of temples there, too, besides the Judaic temples. Is this true?

A: *I hear about other beliefs, or other schools that they call temples.*

D: Have you ever been to those temples?

A: *No, no.*

D: Do you know what Romans are?

A: *Yes. And they have their own buildings, their own schools, their own places of worship. We try to keep as much to ourselves and away from them as possible.*

D: I can understand that. Do you ever see any soldiers?

A: *Not very often. Not around our area, unless they are doing a search for someone.*

D: Is there a market in Jerusalem?

A: *Yes. There is a main area of town. And there is a marketplace. And you can buy anything you might need there. It 's a particular area of town. And there are little... they are all set up. With wares and food and... they are just little lines up and down this area that they call a marketplace. It 's outside.*

D: Is that near where you live?

A: *Yes. I walk to the marketplace. There 's more than one marketplace in this city, but there 's one not too far from us.*

D: These gates in this wall, what do they look like?

A: *Well, I have been told that they have changed. But right now, they are made of wood, and they are two doors that open. And they are tall, very tall and heavy.*

D: If they have changed, what were they before?

A: *I have been told they had to be rebuilt, so they were built taller and stronger.*

D: Why were they rebuilt?

A: *I think there was a problem one time with soldiers. And they were going to teach the people of our Temple a lesson. There was a rebellion because the Romans wanted us to supply them with more grain. And we had had dry years. So there was a rebellion, and they destroyed part of that wall and part of the Temple. I think part of the Temple was rebuilt. The Romans have given us many problems with their laws, and their lack of understanding.*

D: Are the Romans rulers or what?

A: *Yes, they have control. But for us, for people who are of the Temple of Judaism, we feel the ruler is the rabbi. But the Romans have other laws and other power and control.*

D: I think you told me once that you also have a king?

A: *The Roman. The king controls, decrees everyone. The*

Roman king.
D: I suppose as a girl, you would not really have to know much of this anyway.
A: *No, I choose not to. I choose not to acknowledge most of them, from the little bit I have known or heard. I don't really care to know about them, or their laws. They have caused us many hardships. I want to put my energy into living a life of teaching and learning, for the good of all. So people can live together, whether they are Roman or Jewish or of the other beliefs.*
D: But as a country, you have to obey what the Romans say?
A: *Yes. We have been living peacefully for a while now.*
D: That is good. Thank you for telling me that information, because I wondered about the condition in the country. You said you are waiting for the Nazarene to come? What are you doing in preparation?
A: *I am just doing daily routine, but I feel that he will be here with us very soon. And I am ready. I have robes to wear, and I am ready to leave. And the country is not all that safe. Any time you get out of the city or away, there could be — whether they are Roman or not Roman — bands of people that would steal and kill.*
D: So it's not really safe out there, is it?
A: *Not always. We just don't know.*
D: Is that why you want to disguise yourself as a boy?
A: *So I will be more accepted.*
D: Not necessarily because you would be safer?
A: *Right.*
D: Do you think they wouldn't accept these things from a woman?
A: *They would have more difficulty. Women aren't allowed the education of men. They are supposed to take care of the home and the smaller children, so that's what I have done. And I have helped my mother with children she takes care of during the day.*
D: This is all that is expected of a woman, so they think you couldn't have much knowledge. Now let's move ahead in time until he is there, when he arrives, and we will find out what's going to happen. Do I need to count, or are you already there?
A: *No, I see him. (Pause) He's with three other men. And he comes in and he's talking with my father in his shop.*

And... he's now coming in. He greets me. And I let him know that I have made my decision. And that there's only one thing for me to do in this life, and that is to walk with him. And teach and be of service to any of those he wishes me to help with, whether they be ill or poor or in need of anything

D: What does he say?

A: (Pause) *He looked at me, and took my face in his hands, and with those eyes that go beyond this world, he knows... he knows nothing he can say will stop me. And he says, so shall it be. And my mother has now come in. I must tell mother and father now. And I tell them I have done my best, but in this time that has passed and I have been so quiet, I have prayed and I know what God wishes me to do. I have listened to those voices I hear. And I know that no man can find any happiness with me. That it would break my heart to stay here and try to marry and have a family, because that's not my calling. So I hope they will understand, and find love in their hearts for me. But I must be on this journey.*

D: How do they react?

A: *Mother is crying. And father has become quiet. But the Nazarene says, 'This woman child speaks from her heart, and knows the only truth there is. So shall it be. She may walk by my side in peace knowing my protection and love. And she will aid me and learn to live with God's Laws, and to be of service wherever she is needed'.*

D: And if he wants you to go, there's not really much they can say, is there?

A: *No. I think because I was patient and quiet these past months, they know I will do this anyway.*

D: They know it's not just a childish impulse.

A: *Right. And he knows I will walk with him.*

D: When is he going to leave?

A: *In the morning he's heading into the country, into an area where people are very ill and need to hear his teachings, so they may find faith and hope and a reason to go on. And these people, he says, are called 'lepers'. They have a disease that is very sad.*

D: Do you think you will be able to go into an area like that, with so many sick people?

A: *Yes. This was why I am here.*

D: Are others going with him?

A: *He has a group that's usually with him. The group seems to vary in size, But most of his followers are men. Every now and then I see women, but they're older women.*

D: No one your age.

A: *Right. So I am ready.*

D: Then you will leave in the morning. Have you already cut your hair? You said you were going to cut your hair to disguise yourself?

A: *I will do that once I think everyone is in bed. I do not want to cause them any more pain. I will miss the children my mother takes care of. They have brought me much joy. But I know my parents have their own work to do, and are where they are supposed to be.*

D: Of course, you can always come back if it doesn't work out.

A: *Yes. We will be back this way.*

D: Alright. Let's move ahead till the morning when you are going to leave with him, and tell me what is happening.

A: (Sigh) *Well... I am brimming over with love and joy. But... it's just a little sad. Because I am saying goodbye to a life I have known, and I am beginning another.* (Sadly) *But I hug my mother and kiss her, and let her know I will be fine. I must do this, and I love her. And my father has tears in his eyes. We hug. And... I just take one last look.* (All this was said with deep-felt emotion. Then resigned, or with resolution:) *So I am ready to go now.*

D: (It was so emotional I felt as if I was intruding). It will be a whole new life, won't it?

A: (A deep sigh:) *Yes.*

D: You have never really been anywhere outside of Jerusalem, so it will be an adventure, too, won't it?

A: (Softly:) *Yes.*

D: Something that young girls usually don't get to do. (I had to get her mind off the sadness). How many are in the group that are going with you today?

A: *Oh, let me see. There seem to be... twelve, counting all of us.*

D: Counting you and Jesus, too?

A: *Yes, yes.*

D: Do you know any of the other people?

A: *They look familiar. Mainly because I have seen them with him, or when I have sneaked to those meetings. But, no.*

D: I imagine before it's over you will know who they are, and you will know their names. You will get to know them all very well probably. I wonder what they think about you coming.

A: *I think they are on a similar path as me, so they will accept me.*

D: You'll have to find food and shelter and things like that, won't you?

A: *Well, this time of year it's usually warm enough to put up little shelters to sleep under. And it seems as if there are jugs of water and food. So I think they must be prepared for the length of time they need to be gone, or have places they know they can stop at.*

D: Are there any animals with you? I wondered how the things were being carried.

A: *Some of them are carried by hand. And I see a pack animal, a... burro seems to be loaded down with some things. And there seems to be a goat, but I don't know if that goat is going with us or not. I think mainly when they need supplies, they know where to stop.*

D: Did you take anything with you?

A: *Yes. I have a cloth sack in which I have various things. I have a blanket and personal things. And just necessities.*

D: I wondered if there were any personal objects or anything that you might not be able to leave.

A: *Well... I...* (she seemed embarrassed) *I have just taken the bare necessities of what I needed. That is as far as... you mean a personal object, a favorite object?*

D: Yes. Something you couldn't leave.

A: *There is an amulet I have, to hold or wear around my neck. It has been with me since I was a child.*

D: What does it look like?

A: *It was forged by my father when I was a child. And it has a symbol... oh, I guess it's a star, a six pointed star. But it's a symbol to me of love and God. And he must have made that for me when I was five years old.*

D: Does it have any significance other than your father giving it to you?

A: *Oh, he put a letter on it, and this letter stands for life. And this is in the center of this star. It's* (phonetic) *Ah-hi.*

The Jewish man who helped me on some of these Hebrew details said the word for life is spelled phonetically: Chai. and is probably the word referred to, even though it is symbolized by two symbols in the Hebrew language. The center of the Star of David is empty, and it was certainly possible to combine two symbols into one to place a design there.

D: That is the name of the letter?

A: *And it means life.*

D: Does the six pointed star have any significance?

A: *This is the Star of David. This is significant in Judaism.*

D: But most amulets don't have the letter?

A: *No. He did that for me.*

D: Then it would be a very personal object to take with you.

A: *Yes. I don't tell most people about this* (embarrassed laugh).

D: Well, it's personal. And I can understand what it means to you. It would be a part of home to carry with you. Is it going to take many days to get where you're going?

A: *I was told this would be a day-and-a-half walk, depending on, I guess, the energy and health of everyone, and the heat and all. But that's what it should probably take.*

D: Do you know what direction you are going from Jerusalem?

A: *Let me see. We seem to be heading... east and south, yes.*

D: What does the land look like in that direction?

A: *Well... right now I see some hills and sand. And as we keep walking, I see green in the distance. I see a few trees in places. But I see a great deal of open spaces of desert.*

D: Then it would be hot. Is that the way the land appears around Jerusalem. too?

A: *Jerusalem, because you have springs and water, you have some green areas and trees, and there are hills. It is not all desert.*

D: It looks as if it will be a hard journey ahead of you. But if you are determined to go, that's very wonderful. Alright. I want to leave and let you continue on your journey.

I then returned Anna to full consciousness. Naomi receded, to await the next time she would be called forth to continue her story.

The significance of what Naomi wanted to do with her life, and the bravery she displayed in leaving her father's house, was not made clear until I did research into the customs of the time. During the time of Jesus the Jews lived strictly by the Law, the Torah, or the Laws of Moses found in the first books of the Old Testament. These rules governed everything in their life, and was a point of dispute between the priests and Jesus. He had been taught to interpret the Law differently and more fairly while he studied with the Essenes. He thought that in the priests' strictness they had forgotten the individual and that circumstances may influence how these rules could be applied. The case of how women were treated in that culture is an example. At Qumran, the home of the Essenes, women were treated as equal to the men. They were taught anything they wanted to learn, and many became teachers. In *Jesus and the Essenes* we discovered that Jesus had many women disciples, a point that has disappeared from the Bible during its many revisions and exclusions.

Jesus spoke to ordinary people in parables. He presented his teachings in analogies patterned after things in their everyday life which they could understand and relate to. Jesus' disciples were taught metaphysical laws of the universe, methods of healing and the performing of so-called "miracles", because they had the training to be able to understand these things. It is debatable whether he found anyone he could share all his knowledge with. The Bible does not give any indication that he ever did. He found that women were more able to grasp his teachings because of their natural intuitive abilities. When the time came for his women disciples to go out and spread the teachings, he knew they would be in more danger than the men, so he paired them with a male companion for their safety. Jesus' respect of women as equals also explains his defense of the prostitute who was in danger of being stoned. All these things caused friction because they were contrary to the teachings of the Law. This can be understood when we know how women were treated in Palestine during that time.

According to the Torah a woman was inferior to a man. Women took no part in public life. It was suitable and expected for women (especially unmarried girls) to stay indoors. They were not supposed to leave the house without escort, and when they did they were expected to remain unobserved in public. Market places and council halls, law-courts, gatherings and meetings, where a large number of people were assembled — in short, all public life — were proper for men, but not for women. During the huge popular feasts, which took place in the Court of Women at the Temple, the crowds were so large that it became necessary to construct galleries for the women, in order to separate them from the men. They could participate in the local synagogue service, but barriers of lattice separated the women's section, and they even had their own special entrance. During the service, women were there simply to listen. A woman had no right to bear witness in legal matters, because the Law concluded that she would be a liar.

Some of these rules were difficult to enforce, for economic reasons. Many women had to help their husbands in their professions, such as selling their wares or working the fields. However, a woman could not be alone in the fields, and it was not customary, even in the country, for a man to converse with a strange woman. This custom was often broken by Jesus, to the astonishment of his male disciples. He openly conversed with women wherever he found them. Rules of propriety forbade a man to be alone with a woman, to look at a married woman, or even to give her a greeting. It was disgraceful for a scholar to speak with a woman in the street.

This understanding of the customs also shows that women risked condemnation and severe censure for daring to flaunt tradition by even coming to hear him speak. Some of this may explain women's attraction to him. Here was a man who treated them differently from the way in which any man had ever treated them before. No wonder they loved him.

Women's education was limited to domestic arts, especially cooking, needlework and weaving, and looking after younger children. The wife and daughters were totally under the control of the man of the house, with no rights at all. The wife's duty was full obedience to her husband, and the children had to put respect for their father before respect for their mother. Up to the age of twelve the father had full power over a girl. She could even be sold into slavery if necessary. At the age of twelve she became a maiden of full age, and the father would arrange a marriage for her. Her ownership and absolute obedience would then be transferred from her father to her husband.

This custom explains why Naomi was so concerned about her fate if she remained in her father's house. The normal age for a girl's betrothal was between twelve and twelve and a half, and the marriage usually took place one year later. Naomi kept saying she was not yet thirteen, and that she did not desire to be married and live a normal life. This was the only future that she could know or expect. She knew if she did not express her desires, unheard of for a female, that she would be trapped into a life that she could not tolerate. This explains why her request to leave the home and follow her uncle, Jesus, was so extraordinary. It surely would not have been granted under normal circumstances. By so openly defying the customs of her people, Naomi showed that she was an unusual young girl. It also explains why she insisted on cutting her hair and dressing as a boy. A young girl was strictly forbidden to be seen in public alone, let alone being allowed to travel with a group of people. She also disguised herself when she snuck out to attend the hidden meetings. These things would be accepted of a boy, but never a girl.

Schools, as I explained earlier, were religious schools for the study and understanding of the Law. Except for reading and writing, nothing else was taught. Education was solely for Jewish boys, and not for girls. Thus a woman would never be allowed to teach. This ruling may seem contradictory to the lifetime of Abigail in the first part of this book, when she was assigned as a teacher at the Temple. But Abigail made it clear that she was not a Jewess, so she was not bound by the rules of the Torah. This may also explain the deeper reasons why the priests seemed to despise her and her wisdom, and why they sought to subjugate her.

Only against this background can we fully appreciate Jesus' attitude towards women. The Gospels speak of women following him, and this was an unprecedented happening in the history of that time. Jesus knowingly overthrew custom when he allowed this to happen. He preached to women and allowed them to participate openly and even ask questions, and John the Baptist baptized them. Jesus was not content with bringing women up onto a higher plane than was the custom, he wanted to bring them before God on an equal footing with men. Everything Jesus taught was contradictory and radical from the viewpoint of the average person of the time. It took much bravery for men and women both to come to his meetings and to choose to follow his new type of religion.

Chapter Seven

The Village of the Lepers

Leprosy is a very ancient disease dating from Biblical times and probably before. In its worst form it is truly horrible, and even today victims are isolated in hospitals, colonies and islands. Much of this stems from the fear associated with the disease, since it is contagious, and the symptoms can create unfortunate physical conditions that persist for several years before eventually killing the patient.

It is now called Hansen's disease, and it is still not understood exactly how the germ enters the body, or how it is transmitted. It is infectious, but the incubation period is estimated to be from two to twenty years. It is very slow-acting. Even though leprosy is viewed as contagious, often members of the same family do not contract the disease. So even though leprosy has been around since the beginning of known history, it is still a mystery disease.

It is difficult for people of our day to understand the terror and fear that the disease created among the people in Jesus' time. It was so horrible that the only solution was to isolate the victims, separating them in a place apart from the rest of the population. There they could live but would not have to be observed by others. If people could not see them, they could forget about them. In Jesus' time suffering was thought to be a sign of God's displeasure. Thus the people did not care what happened to these poor specimens of human beings, as long as they did not have to associate with them. The Bible calls them "unclean", and people lived in fear of contracting the disease. The unhappy victims could not be cured by ordinary means, and were shut out from society, civilly dead. Their villages were shunned as much as the individuals.

The Bible describes the symptoms of this disease and the precautions to be taken, but the descriptions are vague. Today most Biblical scholars agree that leprosy designated any blemish which marked the victim as "unclean" under Hebraic Law. Medical experts claim some of the symptoms not only describe leprosy but a host of other more common skin diseases, which are neither contagious nor life-threatening. Some of these diseases were a variety of psoriasis, an ancient and very common skin disease. It is the most universal of all skin diseases, being found in every climate and among all races. In some cases among the poor and those living in unclean conditions psoriasis was associated with other infectious disorders, especially scabies or itch. It can rapidly assume a pustular form and give rise to ulceration, thus imitating a symptom of leprosy.

There are also several kinds of skin diseases, which are produced by vegetable parasites or epiphytes. The common ringworm is a well-known example of such disease. None of these impair general health. There are also various fungi, such as those which cause common moldiness and dry rot, which are self-propagating, and affect houses and garments. This is probably what the Bible defines as leprosy in the house or raiment. These give the appearance of some varieties of psoriasis, and are contagious.

There could also have been diseases in Biblical times which are now unknown to us. Many people with various skin afflictions in the Middle Ages and even later were often erroneously considered to be leprous, and treated as such by confinement in leper hospitals. This was done to such an extent that at the beginning of the 16th century an inspection was undertaken of the overcrowded leper hospitals in France and Italy. The greater number of them, and in some instances all of the inmates, were found to be suffering merely from various skin diseases, and only a minority from true leprosy.

Thus it was possible for people with non-contagious and non-life-threatening diseases to be placed in the same category and exiled to isolation with the lepers. The Jews didn't take any chances, and anyone with a persistent skin problem was de-clared "unclean". Fear prevailed, and no one would think of approaching a leper, much less touching one. The lone exception was Jesus, because he accepted everyone as equal. He could see beneath the disfigured outer appearance and knew there was an indestructible human soul dwelling within that deformed body.

True leprosy is normally a slow and insidious disease. In the beginning two distinct features are manifested: loss of sensitivity of the nerve fibers supplying the skin and a congested state of minute vessels under the skin, showing itself in the form of circular spots or blotches of irregular forms and varying extent, on the forehead, the limbs and body, the face and neck perhaps showing only a diffused redness. These blotches can change color, and thus there may exist at the same time red, purplish or white spots. In the early stages there is scarcely any pain, and a certain degree of numbness or anaesthesia exists in all the affected spots. The fingers especially become numb, wasted and brown. There are a number of sores that ulcerate and discharge.

In other cases, joints are dislocated and fingers and toes fall off. Eventually limbs are lost and severe disfigurement of the face and body is created, as bone and cartilage are attacked and destroyed. There is massive physical destruction from this disease, as it slowly and gradually eats away at every part of the body. In many instances almost all trace of the human form may be destroyed by mutilation and disfigurement. While the loss of common sensation is pronounced, there are often internal burning and neuralgic pains that produce great suffering. The miserable victims can live ten or fifteen years as the disease progresses, and there is no known cure that is truly effective. Symptoms can be treated, but the disease itself is incurable. Chaulmoogra oil has been the established treatment of leprosy for centuries. In our time, despite new drug developments, chaulmoogra oil and its derivative ethyl esters continue to be widely used in many parts of the world. This oil comes from seeds of the fruit of a large tree in India. It is quite possible that this oil was known and used in Palestine, because of active trade with surrounding countries, including India.

In the New Testament twelve cases of leprosy are mentioned, and ten must be considered under one heading. In *Luke* 17:12-19, Christ healed the ten lepers, and one returned to give thanks. Nowhere in the New Testament does it mention that Jesus went into the isolated villages especially created for the lepers. There are only these few incidents where he encountered them by chance. Maybe this explains why he was not repulsed or frightened by them. He had, according to my own researches with Naomi, spent much time in their midst in their homes.

I have gone into so much detail because I believe an understanding of this disfiguring disease will make the conditions Jesus and his followers worked in more vivid.

When Naomi said the first place Jesus' group would go to was the village of the lepers, I began to see the logic in Jesus' thinking. He had come to the realization that his niece was determined to go with him. He would not be able to talk her out of it. But it would be "baptism by fire" to take her to a place such as a leper colony. Here she would be exposed to pitiful people with an illness in the worst possible form. It would either make her or break her. She would realize that this type of work was not enjoyable, but it meant being exposed to people's suffering and deliberate isolation. This was no accident that Jesus chose to take Naomi into such a situation and expose her to the worst first. He probably reasoned that if she could not take it, she would beg to be returned to the safety of her parent's home. I believe he would have arranged for her to go back, but in such a case it would be her decision and she would have to live with it. She would have no one to blame but herself. She had followed her heart, and she would soon discover whether or not the path of the Nazarene was her path.

When we continued the story at the next week's session, I assumed that nothing interesting could happen on the day-and-a-half journey. For this reason I moved Naomi ahead to the completion of the trip.

D: The first journey after leaving your parents home is almost over. What are you doing? What do you see?

A: *We are entering the village of the lepers. And I see a large pond of water, and I see hills. The village is protected by the limestone hills. We are entering the village now.*

D: Did you have a hard journey?

A: *It was long and very warm, but we did not meet with any trouble, so it was not that difficult.*

D: Do the others in the group know you are really a girl?

A: *No, they think I am a young boy. I am dressed in the robes of a young boy. And even though my face looks a bit feminine, at this age it's very difficult to tell. I am on the thin, wiry side, so it's a good disguise for a boy.*

D: Are you going by a different name?

A: *I haven't... let me see.* (Chuckle) *I remember now. I hadn't thought about it, but of course, there were so many things on my mind. I was introduced and the Nazarene hesitated. But then he introduced me as Nathaniel. Nathan.*

D: Nathan. Did he tell them you were related in any way?

A: *No, he called me the son of a dear friend, who was trying to find out if this was the right path to be on.*

D: That was very diplomatic. I wondered what the others in the group knew about you? Then he is going to consider you to be Nathan or Nathaniel at this time. You said this village was protected by the hills?

A: *Yes. Let me see if I can explain this. There is a small set of limestone hills, which aren't very high. And at the base of these hills is this village. The pond might be from a large spring. It's on the other side of the village. This is a small colony. There seems to be a little plant life, but the area is fairly dry and desolate.*

D: Is this a long way from other villages or towns?

A: *Yes. They chose this location because of its distance. These people are not treated well, and they needed a place where they could live in relative peace.*

D: Why aren't they treated well?

A: *This disease creates deformities and much fear in other people. So the average person is not friendly and can barely look at these people, especially when the disease has really become critical. They live in fear of getting this disease.*

D: Have you ever seen people with this disease?

A: *No. I don't really feel fear because I feel I am where I am supposed to be. And my voices and my prayers have given me strength to know that I am to be of service. And knowing that I am helping to heal, whether physically or emotionally, gives me strength.*

D: I suppose it would also give you strength, if Jesus doesn't mind going in there.

A: *Yes. His lack of fear dissolves any fear I might have.*

D: And you said there were several others in the group, didn't you?

A: *Yes. Let me see if I can count them. There seem to be about... twelve.*

D: Are they all men?

A: *There are two older women. I think these are women who have backgrounds in healing. They have been on other journeys with him. Maybe they come specifically when he goes to this village.*

D: Do you think he has been to this village before?

A: *Yes, he has. He revisits various locations. They live in hopes of his return.*

D: Do you have any idea how long you will stay there?

A: *I seem to think seven days will pass.*

D: Are you going to live among the people while he is there, or do you know?

A: *We set up our own camp, but it's in the village. And then I am to be by his side, and be taught by the physicians. I will just be an observer or an assistant.*

D: Then some of the group are physicians?

A: *Yes. I know the ladies have been present for births and helped with that. But they have assisted physicians, so they have that knowledge in their background.*

D: Do you think any of the men are physicians?

A: *Not really trained, not this time. He cannot always get physicians willing to come when he's ready to make the journey. These people have the knowledge of working with these lepers, and maybe have been assistants to the physicians, so they can carry on.*

D: Then normally when he makes these journeys, he will take physicians with him.

A: *Yes, if they are available, and willing.*

D: Yes, I can understand that even a physician would be afraid. Then will you move ahead a little and tell me what happens?

A: (Sigh) *Yes. Well, there are three of us going into one little house. The family in the house is an older man and a wife, and there seem to be two other people there. The older man...* (she gave a sharp intake of breath and a sound of revulsion). *Ohhh, boy!*

It was obvious Naomi was having her first exposure to someone stricken with the worse stages of the disease.

A: *I'm trying to be very strong but...* (softly) *it's difficult. He's in very critical condition. It seems that all that can be done now is to try to ease his pain, and hopefully he will make the transition out of his body soon.*

D: You said there were three of you who went in there. Was Jesus one of them?

A: *Yes, and one of the older ladies. She has a parcel with bandages and different powders she can mix to help soothe some of the soreness. It's soothing but nothing seems to really conquer the disease. Since I have been here I have seen it in such different stages. And every now and then it gives you hope it won't get worse. But these people do the best they can to live with faith and help one another.*

D: You said this man is so bad that they will just try to ease his pain. Is the woman going to do that?

A: *Yes, but she is here to mainly bandage and try to soothe the worst of the decay. Jesus is praying and laying his hands upon the man. And... it's almost as if I can see a light emanating from this man's face. The Nazarene placed his hands on the top of the head, the crown, and I see this glowing light. And then he places his hands on the man's heart. He stays this way in silent prayer over the man. And I see this golden glow from his heart area. (Emotionally:) Oooh! It's hard to describe.*

D: What do you mean?

A: *It's beautiful, but it's **more** than that. It fills you up. It fills up any emptiness inside you. And it makes everything feel warm and loved, and there is no emptiness within. It is hard to put it into words.*

D: You mean you feel this way just by watching him?

A: *Yes, yes. And you can tell that this man... his face is at ease... the pain seems to be much less. And the Nazarene the other day... he lifted my hand, and with a finger he drew a circle in my palms* (she went through these motions). *And he said, 'This, too, is the heart. The center of your palms. In the center is another heart chakra'. And that's why there is so much power in the healing of these hands, because of that energy coming straight through.*

D: Did he use the word 'chakra'?

A: *Heart... center. Heart... chakra? I'm not sure.*

D: Did he mean **your** hands, or his own?

A: *I think he meant **everyone's** hands. He took my hand... and he took the other one, and he said, 'These, too, are heart centers'.* (She again went through the motions of drawing circles on the center of her palms).

D: He drew a circle in your palms?

A: *Yes. Maybe this is just part of my teaching, because I have always felt the energy and the strength there. And every time he would touch me it was so strong. So maybe if you know the connection, if you are aware of the connection, and it's done through the heart and with purity, then the energy is just a direct connection. And that energy from the heart is the strongest medicine of all.*

D: Many people wouldn't understand that, would they?

A: *I guess not, but it just seems so natural to me.*

D: Then he means that in addition to the heart inside your body, there are also other heart centers in the body?

A: *That's how he explained it. That's what I understood, and I never heard anyone say anything like that before.*

D: Maybe this explains some of the ways he is able to heal.

A: *When he told me it just seemed so right. It made so much sense. And then when I watched him, it was all so clear. And when you look at the people, you know this is a tool. This poor man was in such desperate pain, and his face is so at peace right now.*

D: Do you think the others in the room can feel the same thing you feel?

A: *I don't know. I know they must feel something, because... the silence is so different. They must feel the energy, or just see the love and caring flowing from him.*

D: I think it would be obvious to anyone who watched him that this is not an ordinary man.

A: *No. He is so* **aware,** *so in tune with his...* (she had difficulty finding the words). *God's connection, or God within him, or God purpose. I don't know the right word. But I guess most people wouldn't even be aware of things that are so clear and so simple to him.*

D: Do you think he is different from other men?

A: *He is different because of his sensitivity and understanding, and his total lack of fear. He is so* **sure** *of his place and duty.*

D: Have you ever heard anyone say that he might be different from other men?

A: *Yes. There are people that turn him into something that is more like a god. He has powers and capabilities such as I have never seen. I know he is of flesh, but yet I know his spirit and energy is different.*

D: You have heard people say they think he's more like a god?

A: *Yes. Because when you see him do some of the things he does, there's no other way to explain it. And yet he tries hard to teach that we all are capable of being what he is and doing what he is doing. Except that I believe most of us can't find the purity of heart and desire. It's very hard to be on a path like his, and not be drawn off by other things that most men and women are drawn off by.*

D: Yes. The human part of living would make it very difficult to remain pure. In that way he is different.

A: *In that way he **is** like no one else.*

D: I wonder what he thinks if he hears people say he is like a god?

A: (Laugh) *But he doesn't accept that. Oh, I can remember him saying — it's something like this — he said, 'My brother, I am no more than you. I only recognize what I can be and how I can serve. And I have true love and faith in my God'. He tries to clarify what he thinks his purpose is.*

D: What does he think his purpose is?

A: *He thinks he was sent here to be a teacher of life, a ray of life. To be an example of what humankind **can** be, and of the gifts humankind has. And that people can all do what he is trying to teach them.*

D: That makes sense to me, but you know how people are. It's very hard to get through to some of them.

A: *Yes. And most people live in such fear of **something**, or **many** things. Until they can dispel this fear and not be afraid of knowing themselves and listening to their heart, then they will not be reached. They have to find it themselves.*

D: Yes, that makes sense. (I returned to the scene she was watching:) But he's working with this man in the room, and then the man is no longer in pain. Does he do anything else in that little house?

A: *No. He was with the man a while and then he went over to the wife, and just held her hands. I couldn't quite hear what he said to her, but he said he would return. And he was going on to the next visit.*

D: Do you go with him on that visit, too?

A: *Yes. We went... Oh, this is very sad. The next building we went into housed children who were without family or parents. You see, not all of these children appear sick. You can't tell that they have the disease. I guess you could develop this disease in various stages or at different ages. So some of them are so perfect looking. And then some of them are so... eaten away* (a deep sigh). *But this is the house of the children.*

D: They live in that house together, the ones that have no parents?

A: *Yes. There is a nurse or nurse-caretaker that stays with them all the time. And there are other helpers or attendants that come in during the day.*

D: What does he do there?

A: *He goes to each child and... either talks to them or... He always touches. I see him touching the face, smiling lovingly, and then placing his hands on them. But he takes time to talk to each of them.*

D: Can you hear what he's saying?

A; *Oh. There's a little girl sitting in a corner and... he asks her name and...* (smiling broadly) *she got upon his lap. And she asks him if she will be well or will she die. And he tells her that she will be well, and that she will grow up and help take care of the children. And that she must have a pure heart, a loving heart, and not despair, because she is where God needs her. And she will know love and... that's what he says to her* (this was all said with such beautiful emotion).

D: That's very beautiful. What did the little girl do?

A: *She's just sitting staring at him. And he hugged her and put her down. And she's smiling. And there's a boy he's going over to, who has just one leg. And oh, he's in very bad shape* (big sigh). *But Jesus is going over and kneeling beside the boy, and putting his hands on the boy. And his little face is looking up, and the tears are running down his cheeks* (she was almost in tears herself as she related this). *But the child recognizes something special. I can tell.*

It was difficult for me to remain objective. The narrative was so moving, I truly felt that I was actually there in the presence of all this heartfelt emotion.

D: Could you see anything this time? I was thinking of that light.

A: *Oh. I saw... I seem to always see the light. Maybe not as strongly as I did before. There was something very strong with that older man. But I always see a little glow coming from the hands of the Nazarene whenever he places his hands. This time I saw the glow when he put his hands on the boy's head, and his heart, and his legs. But I also see the glow, the **golden** glow, around Jesus' head... like a little half circle.*

D: Is that always there?

A: *No, not always. It's there sometimes when he's with someone, or sometimes I will see it when he is looking at me. But it's not always there.*

D: Did anything happen when he put his hands on this little boy?

A: *Well, it eased him. It always seems to ease people. But that's what I saw.*

D: Then a miracle does not always occur each time he does this, or how would you define a miracle?

A: *I think the fact that the pain is eased and they are at peace, I would call a 'miracle'. But you don't see these people, who are this ill, get up and walk and have their bodies grown back together. The miracle is the love and how it eases them. And if they are meant to get better, they do. I have heard stories that some of these people never get the disease. And sometimes it stops, and they don't know why. But usually it progresses, and all you can do is ease the pain.*

D: Then it takes different forms in different people.

A: *Yes. And sometimes if his energy is accepted... maybe it's the people that have more faith or more strength in the things they feel coming from him, maybe these people have an easier time. Although, he told me that everybody has their time to be returned to the Source. They might just be in this physical body for a while, so it's difficult to know.*

D: That makes sense. Does he have any explanation for why people have to suffer in that way?

A: *He believes it is part of the progression of the individual. It's very difficult to explain when you see people in such pain and being eaten away. But he knows that reasons exist for everything, and lessons are to be learned from everything, so nothing happens by accident. Maybe they created this learning in a prior time, when they walked here in another form. That is why people in pain or with disease are sometimes allowed to go sooner than others, because the lesson is over with.*

D: Does he think that human beings have lived in other forms?

A: *He doesn't say it **exactly** that way, but he says, 'When they have been here before. When they have learned **prior** lessons'. He says it in different ways. But you understand that he believes we visit this land more than once, for the learning and for being of service. And that we are on God's mission every time we come. It is to help us learn and get closer to where we, as a people, are supposed to be. So there is no separation.*

D: Is this the same thing that your religion teaches?

A: *No. I have never heard things in my background that I have heard from him. And yet when I hear it from him, it sounds so clear, so right, so familiar. I know he studied in many places with many wise teachers. So he has been made aware of so much more.*

D: Yes, so much more than the average rabbi.

A: *Yes. They do not want to hear anything new. So he walks his own path, and teaches his own beliefs.*

D: Maybe this is one of the reasons he doesn't always agree with the Temple.

A: *Yes. And it fills the rabbis with distress and fear that their beliefs would be shaken. That their power and authority would be questioned. And he is able to do this in a way where he doesn't have to be powerful and violent. So I have learned there are many kinds of fear, and you cannot see clearly or feel the truth or the light. You have to peel off each layer of fear. And I guess that could take many lifetimes.*

D: Then I can see that the rabbis would be afraid of him. The average person wouldn't challenge their authority, would they?

A: *No, because you are raised with the teaching that 'This is the truth. This is the Law, and you do not question it or challenge it'.*

D: They must think he is a very unusual person, to challenge them.

A: *Yes. Most of them, not all of them. There are some that are wiser and kinder. They won't speak up for him, but they won't go against him.*

I returned to the scene she was watching.

D: Does he do anything else in the house with the children?

A: *Oh, he is just visiting with them and later on they will go out and sit with him by the spring. Or the ones that can might walk with him.*

D: That's very good. Did you do anything else on that day?

A: *Oh. I went with the older woman on some of her* (unsure of the word) *chores, and assisted with bandages and mixing powders. I just helped to clean up and make things comfortable for the people.*

D: Then you didn't stay with Jesus the entire time. There are many other things to be done, too. Well, it sounds as if you are doing what you wanted to do. Are you glad you came, or are you sorry?

A: *Oh! I am very glad. This is what I am supposed to do. I am very sure of this. I have no desire to do anything else. As I have said, to have stayed in my parents' home and to have married and tried to have a family, I would have disappointed many people. Because if you go against your heart and your intuition, it reaches you eventually. Then you have to face it, and usually everyone suffers. So it's better to be truthful, and maybe cause a little pain in the beginning. But to know what your truth is and where you should be is always the best.*

D: I thought that as a young girl who hadn't been out in the world very much, it would be hard for you to see people who are so horribly sick.

A: *It is hard, because even my imagination never quite made it seem this way. But there is this overpowering sense of being needed and useful. And in the giving, as the receiving, this fills me up. I don't need anything else.*

D: That's good, because many young girls would want to go home after seeing something like that.

A: *No. For me I want to reach out more. I want to ease them in every way I can.*

D: That's very admirable.

A: *No. I don't know how to explain it. I could not have done* *anything else in this life. **I** need **this**. I need this as much as anyone I might help, because there's nothing else to fill me up.*

D: Alright. Well, let's move to the days ahead, and see if there is anything that happens while you are there in the village that you want to tell me about. An event or something that Jesus does that you want to talk about. Can you find an incident?

A: *I see a more pleasant time where we are gathered around the spring. It's a very pleasant day, and he has many of the people of the village outside with him. I see him standing there with his hands raised, and he is talking. And he goes over and gets a little cup of water... and he gives it to one of these women sitting there. She drinks the water. And he lays his hands on her head. He said to her, 'My sister, the light of God is on you. This energy is flowing through you. You will find strength, and you will release this disease. For you are needed in another capacity'. And I see the lady sitting there in a trance... I feel a cool breeze... And I remember time going by. He sat down across from her. And I see his hands lifted like this* (she raised her hands so the palms were facing outward). *I see that glow from his heart and around his head, and in his hands, in the center of his palms. She opens her eyes. And there is a different, more calm look about her... And she's crying. She takes his hand and kisses it, and thanks him, for she knows a change has come over her. She said she heard a voice speak to her. And she knows that her place is to be in the village, and to be trained as a physician so she can help heal and comfort those who need her.*

D: Do you think she has been healed of the disease?

A: *I can tell that she appears different to me. There is something visible in the look about her. There is a calm look. A different kind of a glow. There is a change but I can't really tell. I know that her legs had been affected, but I don't know, inside of her, how badly she had been affected. So we will see. But this is not the same person.*

D: I wondered if she had some visible sign of the disease that had changed?

A: *It was on her legs, I remember, and she had trouble walking. But I haven't seen her get up or move. She is just sitting in that same place, having kissed his hands, and I am seeing the tears flow. Tears of love and joy. But the face, the look is different. Something definitely changed the person. I think sometimes physical changes occur slower; they don't always happen immediately. The immediate thing was the totally different look of her. The peaceful look, the glow.*

D: Maybe the physical change will happen slowly over a longer period of time.

A: *This, I've heard, happens. And I am hoping that this will happen for her.*

D: Then sometimes he doesn't just take the pain away. He works in different ways.

A: *Yes. He says everybody has their own purpose, their own plan. And these people need all the strength of one another to carry on. If they can see that within their own village people can regain themselves and be of help, that is healing in itself for the others.*

D: Yes, it is. Then you think he is able to see what their path is?

A: *I think sometimes he can, or sometimes when he touches people, I think he gets clear pictures or clear thoughts. And he knows immediately what they are supposed to do. The clarity comes.*

D: Apparently he could tell that this woman was supposed to do something else.

A: *Yes. I don't see it always happen that way. Or sometimes things will happen and we will not even hear about them. There's no plan to it. It happens at different times; there's no regular pattern.*

D: After you leave, something could happen, too, and you wouldn't even know about it. That's what you mean. Alright. Let's move ahead to another incident that happened while you were there. Did anything else interesting happen?

A: (Pause) *Well, that was very special. But I... Oh, yes! I saw him take the bandages and the powders and place them on the face of a man whose cheeks were being eaten away. He did this, and then he kept his hands there and prayed. And when we came back to check on this man the next day, the change was...* (sigh) *It's hard to talk about because it just doesn't seem real.* (In awe:) *It was... as if the cheeks had grown back. The disease was still there, but I had never seen the powders work like that when the women used them. It always helps. It always soothes the pain — and especially if it's bad infection, it can make a big difference. But this man was moving his mouth and drinking without any pain, and there was... a changed look, like with that lady. And I guess, maybe sometimes the Nazarene will know that... maybe he gets a clear thought or picture. Maybe he knew that even though this is this man's path, the man had already made much progress spiritually. Maybe somehow with his heart energy connecting with the Nazarene, it is so strong that it affects the physical. And this man's face was grown back together, although the disease was still there. But he was like a different person, with a different look to him. He was able to move and use his mouth, and he could do this without any pain. So this was a great miracle. They are all miracles. I guess anything could be a miracle.*

D: It just doesn't happen the same way every time.

A: *No. And you are scared — not really — maybe that's not the right word. But to talk about having seen something like that, almost makes it less real. Sometimes if you keep it to yourself you know it's safe, and it will remain the way you saw it.*

D: Because it's so hard to believe.

A: *But that was... so* **special**.

D: Is everyone that he comes in contact with helped, or are there some people who are not helped at all?

A: *I think everybody is eased. Oh, it doesn't always last. But you can see the pain is eased when he visits them and touches them. It is rare when the disease is changed, but they are always at ease even if it is just for a little while.*

D: I wondered if there were some people that weren't helped at all.

A: *Oh. I think there could be, but I haven't seen that. I have seen him place his hands and talk to these people. It seems to have helped even if it has been for a short while.*

D: Then they are all helped in different degrees. Were you there in the village for seven days as you expected?

A: *Yes. We were there for seven days.*

D: What did you do after that?

A: *We are on a journey to another village.*

D: I wondered if you were returning home?
A: *No. I think this journey this time is going to be for three more seven-day periods. He has certain areas he is going to visit.*
D: Do you know anything about what you will find in the next place?
A: *It is a village where he has many followers. Where they ask him to come and lecture and tell his word.*
D: Is it very far?
A: *Let me see... this will be two days.*
D: Did you hear any of the men's names in the group that you have been with all this time?
A: *Yes. There is... John, Ezekiel and Jeremiah... David* (pause as she thinks). *I'm not sure.*
D: Now that you have been among them, I thought you would know some of their names. You told me what the women did. What were the other men doing during this time?
A: *Well... you see, I didn't come in contact with many of these people. I guess some of them helped with repairs and building, and some of them are scribes and teachers. Some of them I really have spent no time with at all, or I haven't even seen. So... I think they have specific duties, different ways of helping. Some of them will go off by themselves and pray or study, so I don't see them all the time.*
D: That makes sense, because there must be many ways of helping in a village where everyone is so sick. Repairs couldn't be made, so the men could help in that way. And if they were teachers they probably were working in other parts of the village.

This sounded very practical. The interpretation of the Biblical stories of Jesus and his disciples gives the impression that they followed him from place to place listening and trying to learn from him. To me, this version sounds more like what might have actually taken place. It would be commonsense for Jesus to surround himself with people who had many talents, so they could work with the people they came in contact with in practical ways. After all, they were all living in the real world that was full of hardships. It also shows that Jesus did not expect to perform miracles constantly. He took physicians (men and women) with him to use their healing powders and potions. He did not rely on his powers alone. Our Biblical version has always painted him as being omnipotent, needing no one. I believe he was much more human than we have ever given him credit for. If he needed no one, then he could have repaired the buildings miraculously also. The disciples and followers did all they could to help, and did not sit idly by watching the master perform his works.

D: It sounds as if Jesus surrounds himself with many different kinds of people on his journeys.

A: *Yes. They usually seek* **him** *out also. Many of them feel a need to be of service and to give, in the capacity that they can do best. So they always seem to be there at the right time, and he ends up with the people he needs.*

D: Does John have any particular duties?

A: *He seems to be very close to Jesus, and he seems to try to be the other eyes and ears for him. He keeps things connected so people who need to see him get to see him and to be sure he gets to the gatherings. John organizes many of the activities or meetings.*

D: You mean he goes ahead of the group and sets these things up?

A: *Sometimes he does that, depending on the type of journey. But once we get to a location, he seems to keep our schedule organized, making sure things get done, and bringing to the attention of the Nazarene anything he needs to know.*

D: Then he'll know when someone wants to have a meeting or a gathering.

This was another practical idea not presented in the Bible. John was similar to a public relations man. Jesus could not just wander from village to village: he needed someone to go ahead and make sure everything was ready, and to check that everything was safe.

D: The village you are going to, where you said there are groups of his other followers, does this village have a name, or have you ever heard it called anything?

A: *It sounds like... Bar-el* (she repeated it and I said it after her).

D: And you will be there in two days. This will be different. There won't be so many sick people there. Well, he started

you out by showing you the worst, didn't he?
A: *Yes. Which is okay, you know.*
D: Maybe the wisdom behind that was, if you couldn't take it he would know right away (we both laughed). Is it alright if I come again and speak with you? Because I enjoy listening to your journey and to your stories. I want to learn, too.
A: *So do I.*
D: And I want to learn as many things as I can about this man, so you're helping me also.

I then brought Anna back to full consciousness. I left the tape recorder running as she told me some of the things she remembered of the session.

A: *I am remembering that the people that don't get well or don't get any better have no anger towards the ones that do. Right now, with the memory still being this clear, I'm getting a very strong feeling about that.*
D: There was no resentment?
A: *No. And for some reason that thought just came into my head, because right now I'm finding it unusual.*
D: Well, the whole thing is unusual! (laugh).
A: *Maybe it was enough that* **any** *of the people who came in contact with him knew that* **ease***, that sense of being filled up... even if it was just for a short while. And maybe having contacted that feeling gave them enough joy for their fellow man, that it did away with any kind of resentment that might have been there.*
D: This is showing that everything he did was against human nature.
A: *I'm trying to compare this with any other regression we've done. It's the same thing, but this is so much more... involved and emotional, I guess I would say. Maybe some of this is staying with me. I guess every regression has taught me a lesson about something. I feel really good about this one, because I feel very clear about it. I mean, the man was real to me. And I tell you, when I looked at those eyes — I can still feel that — I was so totally filled. I've never known that feeling before, to be so totally full of contentment and love. There has always been this little empty spot in me, and that was gone.*

D: It's gone now?
A: *Well, it's gone when we are working. It's not gone in this life. But... there's always been this little empty nagging spot. When I was with him and looked in his eyes, it was the most complete emotional feeling I have ever had.*

Although Anna expressed it differently, she was describing essentially the same emotion that Mary felt. Apparently this was the wonderful effect Jesus had on people.

A: *When I'm regressed, it's so natural to be there, but then when I'm awake it would be the last thing I would think of. I'm really feeling very emotional, but it's very cleansing. I mean, I feel so relaxed.*
D: Well, you couldn't want for any better feeling.

This was an interesting point that was brought out in this session: the fact that Jesus did not heal every person he met. This concept was also presented in *Jesus and the Essenes.* He was able to ease pain and suffering in the majority of those he came in contact with, but total alleviation of the symptoms and complete restoration from the illness or disability were rare. There were many times when no cure was received, and Naomi made it clear that this was not in Jesus' hands. It was related to the person's karma and destiny in life. Even he could not go against the higher forces controlling such things.

Chapter Eight

The Village on the Sea of Galilee

The following week, as we began the session, I returned Anna (as Naomi) to the time when she was traveling with Jesus.

D: Let's go back to when you left the leper village with the Nazarene and the rest of the group, on the first journey you made with him. You were going to another village where you said he would meet with some of his other followers. I will count to three and we will be there. 1... 2... 3... we are coming into the second village on your travels with the Nazarene. What are you doing?

A: *We are entering a village on a lake. The Lake of Kennaret (phonetic), and we have a meeting of the followers, the believers of this way of life, these teachings. Our stay here, from what I understand, is mainly for purposes of spreading the word and reinforcing our numbers.*

I wrote the name of the lake phonetically. Later when I had a chance to look at a map in the back of my Bible I found the Lake of Kinnereth, also called the Sea of Gennesaret or Chinnereth, a close match to my phonetic spelling. I thought this was remarkable. It is a Jewish name for the Sea of Galilee. I had never known this lake by any other name. I found in my research that in Hebrew and in Aramaic "yam" can mean both sea and lake, and that the Greek translation of the Bible imitates this.

Anna had been having doubts as to the validity of the strange material that was coming from her subconscious during these sessions. After I made this discovery I told her about it, and she did not recognize the name Kinnereth either. I told her it was the old name for the Sea of Galilee. She then asked with a straight face, "What's the Sea of Galilee?" This was totally unexpected. I was momentarily stunned, because I realized the importance of her question. Every Christian knows this Biblical place name because it is so associated with the life of Jesus. This showed beyond a doubt that Anna did not even have a rudimentary knowledge of his life or of the New Testament. When I explained it to her she felt better because it seemed to supply the proof she needed to convince her that this information was definitely not coming from her own mind.

D: Are the people in the town mostly believers, or will you have to be secret here also?

A: *There is a good size group here. We have to keep fairly quiet, but we can feel safe. This is a smaller town, and it seems the people that live here are very much alike in thought. So we can feel safe here.*

D: There isn't as much danger about meeting openly?

A: *No, because there seems to be an understanding here. On the surface they are just a small town, but they are very cautious about the teachings.*

D: Did anyone tell you the name of this town, or does it have a name?

A: *This is the village on Lake Kinnereth.*

D: That's all you know it by? Is there a certain place in the village you're going to?

A: *Yes. There is an area by the lake. First we will go and cleanse ourselves in the lake. This cleansing is necessary for both the body and the spirit. On one portion of the shore there are some very small bluffs. And within these bluffs there are meeting rooms. They are not known to everyone, for they have false fronts. This is where we will be for our meeting, but it seems we will be staying on the banks of the lake.*

I later did research about this area near the Sea of Galilee. There are many places where mountains and bluffs come down practically to the edge of the lake. This was especially true of Magdala (the home of Mary Magdalene), where the shore road winds its way along a steep mountain slope. In the area of Arbeel there are caves that have a history as hiding places for criminals or political refugees during the time of Christ. Some of these were natural caves that were enlarged to be used as places of refuge, and some were so high on the bluffs that they were virtually inaccessible to discovery by soldiers.

During the time of Christ, Galilee was one of the most fertile agricultural areas on Earth. As late as 680AD the Sea of Galilee area possessed great forests. But the fruit trees praised by the historian Josephus have now shriveled to miserable remnants of their old selves. The forests have, for the most part, disappeared, and have been replaced by sparse desert conditions in many places. In Jesus' time the valley had a hot, dismal climate around the lake, because sea breezes were cut off by the mountains. In wintertime the hills and shores would be green, but in the long summer a depressing aridity spread over everything.

It has been proven that people can make the journey on foot from Jerusalem to the Sea of Galilee in three days. The valley would be avoided during the summer because of the excessive heat. Travelling would normally have only been done in winter and early spring when the climate was warm, and sleeping in the open would be possible. At all seasons the Jordan Valley might be a desirable route to persons not wishing to be seen in the towns, for fear of the government or for other reasons.

The Bible states that Cana, in Galilee, was one of Jesus' favorite places. Historians think that Cana was suitable as a center for anyone who wished to organize rebellion, but had powerful enemies in larger towns, and therefore could not make any place a permanent abode. This would be another reason for Jesus' wandering. It was dangerous to stay anywhere very long, unless he knew for sure he would be safe there.

Stories of his accomplishments quickly spread out of Galilee over the whole of Palestine. It was taken for granted that Galilee had close connections with all parts of Palestine, so that information concerning Jesus quickly reached all the corners of the land. Thus those in power in Jerusalem were kept informed of this subversive's activities, but they felt no need to stop him so long as he stayed away from the larger cities. Or unless it became obvious that he was inspiring a rebellion.

Research revealed that there were literally hundreds of small towns and villages in this area that were not recorded by history — or at least no mention of them have passed down to us. There were many large cities existing at the time of Christ that were never mentioned in the Bible, thus it should not be surprising that the smaller ones have disappeared from sight and records. I believe this historical description of the Jordan Valley and the Sea of Galilee fits precisely with the places described by Naomi.

D: I thought you were going to someone's house.

A: *I think for safety they found it best to do it this way. You see, when you have just a handful of people you are able to do that. But there is a large group here.*

D: I think you told me John goes ahead and sets this up?

A: *Yes. I think when they start out on their journeys they have a fairly good idea where each one is going to take them. They might swerve off their path every now and then, depending on the importance. But John usually has things prepared, so things will go as smoothly and as safely as possible.*

D: Then you are going to meet in one of the rooms on this bluff. When is the meeting going to take place?

A: *It seems that this meeting will occur tomorrow in the early morning. We will relax this evening, and at dawn we will meet.*

D: Do you have any problems getting food to eat?

A: *No. We are provided with food and we carry certain provisions with us. We try not to be a burden to anyone. We accept whatever gifts they may wish to give, in the form of food and shelter, but we can be self-reliant.*

D: Then let's move ahead to the morning when the meeting is to take place, and tell me what is happening.

A: *We are being led into this room. And they have covered over the front of one of these bluffs with some stone and some trees. They have done a very good job. And so I see this bluff open up. There are some straw mats on the floor, and there are candle lights. And... there are some wooden benches and tables. The group seems to be a rather good size. About forty people is approximately what I can see.*

And it is good, I see a mixture of men and women.

D: The room will hold them all without being crowded?

A: *Yes, this is a large room. The opening is deceiving... but you enter and it is a large room. They have secured it, propped it up with different materials to make sure it is safe. There seems to be a little hallway, and maybe some other small rooms off to the side.*

D: Is it some sort of natural cave or...?

A: *Yes. It seems as if they just did some clearing out of accumulated earth. And there was a natural... a room in here. And then a natural little path and... it looks as if there could be a few smaller rooms back there.*

D: There are probably not any windows, but there are the candles.

A: *Right.*

D: And these are all people who have come to hear him speak. Can you tell me what happens? Do they have any kind of ceremony or procedure that they go through?

A: *The person who is in charge of this meeting is showing much concern for the Nazarene's welfare. Because they are getting comments from messengers that his teachings are being spread far and wide. And the government is becoming...* **uneasy**.

D: They don't like his popularity?

A: *Yes. Or the idea that people can think for themselves and choose their own path. There are people who are not very fond of him, both in the Temple and in the government. So this group is just talking about their concern, and how to carry on his work. But he rises and he speaks, and he says they should fear not, for he is walking his path directed by God, his path of the heart. And he fears nothing. The only fear he might have is that he might not be able to teach and touch all the people he needs to in his lifetime.*

This was spoken slowly with breaks, as though she was hearing him speak the words and then repeating them to me in broken phrases.

D: Then he has no fear of these rumors or these people who are against him?

A: *No. It will not make any difference in what he does with his life, because he knows he walks with God. And God grows from within. That eternal light is not only in the Temple, but eternal light is in the heart. And that eternal flame never dies, even though you leave the physical being. So he will continue walking and teaching what he believes is right. He will teach what he believes is his reason for existing.*

The eternal light referred to was a light that was never extinguished located in the inner court of the Temple.

D: But they wanted to warn him anyway.

A: *Yes. It seems tensions are mounting, and we hear this kind of rumor every now and then. And then things calm down for a while. And, you know, the government is very fickle. If they get too worried they will just come up with a new tax.*

D: (Laugh) That's their answer.

A: *Yes, it is their way of hurting and manipulating. If there is a special occurrence happening, or if a battle has been won, they will be preoccupied. Things will die down, because the focus will be on something else.*

D: And the priests just go along with what the government says?

A: *The priests? The priests and the rabbis differ. The Roman priests, yes. The rabbis do what they have to do to survive, but they are neither for the government nor for the Nazarene. So....*

D: (Laugh) They're kind of in the middle. They probably think that's the safest place to be. Well, are there any other preparations, or is he just going to speak?

A: *He is speaking now. And... just speaking his heart. He will just linger here a short while and this village seems to be a contact. It seems as if there are many true followers here who will receive their assignments and head out on their own paths. So this is a safe haven, a little bit of relaxation, a communication, and then heading out again. This group seems to be able to spread his teachings, but yet they can also infiltrate into other areas and be accepted as Romans or whatever they need to be in order to protect their teacher.*

D: Then these are people who know his teachings, so he

doesn't have to explain as much to them.

A: *Right. These are followers, dedicated followers.*

D: Then mostly what he is telling them are the things he wants them to do?

A: *Yes. But they also have time for prayer and communication, and the lessons are never over. They have interaction in that way.*

D: I was wondering if there was anything important that he told them that you didn't already know about?

A: *Oh, no, I guess he is mainly just reassuring them that they should not fear. Whatever happens, it is part of his reason for being. And whatever happens in his life or* **to** *him, there is a lesson to be learned there that goes way beyond the surface. He is also trying to remind them to find strength in their own God inside, and look through the heart, and be of service to fellow men and women.*

D: How is he dressed while he's been on this journey?

A: *The usual robes.*

D: Any certain colors?

A: *Oh, the colors are simple. Mainly the tan material. Every now and then there is this stripe that goes through the edge of the garment, the hood and the sleeves and the hem. But otherwise, its very simple.*

D: Then more or less he's dressed like the rest of you?

A: *Oh, yes.*

D: But they are all meeting there today to decide what they are going to do and to get their instructions, so to speak.

A: *Yes. And to keep him aware of progress that is being made. So it's just that.*

D: What kind of progress have they made? Is there anything in particular?

A: *It seems that they travel in their own little groups. And if they hear of a place where there might be interest in the teachings, they go seek out that area. Or if there is somebody in need of help, or who is having much injustice, they will go there. They find ways of using the underground or helping people in whatever way they can.*

D: Then they do more than just spread the teachings.

A: *Yes. Because one of the main teachings is to have love of your fellow human beings, and to treat them as you would like to be treated. There is much misuse of this practice.*

It was becoming obvious that Jesus taught his followers to perform practical services for people, as well as spreading his teachings. This point was also brought out in *Jesus and the Essenes* — that, contrary to the Biblical version, he encouraged his followers to leave him and go out on their own. They did not wait until after his death. He did this so they would not become dependent on him.

D: Is he going to stay there in that village for a while?

A: *I think he would like to linger one more night, but he feels that we should be leaving, so we will be heading out of this village soon.*

D: Then there was nothing else important that happened at that village?

A: *No, just that you should understand that they do spread the teachings. They always appear to go out to do that, but there are other things that they do. They can use that or other things as a disguise for whatever needs to be done, but they always live by the teachings.*

D: Do you know where he is going next?

A: *There seems to be another town. They told me... Giberon?* (phonetic)

The *Bible Dictionary* lists two places that sound like this: Gibeah. a city in the hill country of Judah, and Gibeon, a royal city of the Canaanites. It would seem that Gibeah would more accurately fit the description of the area they were passing through.

A: *It seems there are more followers there, yet they are just starting on their path. It seems wherever he goes he tries to do whatever these people are in need of, with the healing, the teachings.*

D: And the ones at the village by the lake were the more advanced followers. Would that be correct?

A: *Yes. But even there, he is there to be of service, and to help the individuals that seek him out. But it didn't seem as if anything came up in this meeting. I think they are doing quite well right now. I don't think there is any upheaval or any suffering occurring.*

D: Then everything is working the way it should in that village. And in the next village there are supposed to be followers that are more or less starting out and they are not so sure of themselves. Would that be correct?

A: *Yes. And this next village seems quite a bit larger. I guess you could call the Lake Kinnereth village just a small colony. And this is a larger place we are going to.*

D: Will it take long to get there?

A: *I think we could do it by evening, he said. Or if not, by the next day early.*

D: Then it's not very far. Has John also arranged things at that village?

A: *I guess he has. Yes.*

D: Does John go ahead of you, and you don't see him till you get there, or how is that done?

A: *That is how it happens sometimes. I would say usually. But there are occasions when he will come back to either divert us somewhere else, or tell us if there are any changes.*

D: Then he really goes ahead and sets everything up.

A: *Yes, and then we see him again once we are there.*

D: Let's move ahead to when you get to the next village, and tell me what's happening. You said it was a larger village?

A: *Yes. I see a well in the center of a large square. And there is a large area where people come and get water. So this village is more like a small town, the way you see the little center square and small buildings. (Pause) I have been told that I might spend some time here, so I may be of service and learn. It seems that I will be working with somebody who has been on journeys with him before, but is now, I guess you can say, stationed in this village. I guess that's what you might call it. And so I am supposed to be in a learning position here, to help pass on the teachings and care for those who need it. I am just to be of assistance.*

D: And he will go somewhere else while you're there?

A: *Yes. He will come back for me. And then it seems he has to head back towards Jerusalem.*

D: Is anyone else out of your group going to stay there with you?

A: *Not where I will be staying. I think every now and then, depending on what a town or village needs, he might leave some of his followers to assume certain roles. Sometimes they are there for a brief period of time, and sometimes they end up staying. So I think, from what I am feeling, that there are some of the previous followers in this village. Maybe they are working in different capacities, whether at teaching or healing, or just being there for whoever is in need.*

D: How do you feel about him leaving you there?

A : *I feel as if I am ready to stay in one place for a while. If he says this is where I am supposed to be so I may learn and be of service, then it seems very right for me to be here. I am so alive and so filled with what he has allowed me to do and learn from him, but it just seems very natural to have this happen.*

D: Did anything else happen before he left?

A: *He is talking with a few men from the village. And they are scheduling him to stay at different places, and help him visit with those who need him most. Then they will have a gathering in the evening. You see, many of these people of his teachings, and his followers, have managed to build large meeting rooms below their homes, so they can't be found out.*

D: Then he will be talking to these followers who are not as experienced.

A: *Yes. Answering questions, and usually that is where his teachings come in. Or if he feels moved, then he will talk on a significant subject.*

D: Then do you want to move ahead to the night of the gathering, and tell me what is happening?

A: *I have been introduced to the person I will be working with. His name is Abram* (pronunciation with strong Ah sound on first syllable). *I will be staying in his home, and learning further teachings, but also assisting with anything he feels I should be doing. A variety of things, whether it is working with the ill or the older people or the orphans, or just teaching.*

D: Did he introduce you as Naomi or as Nathaniel?

A: (An embarrassed smile) *Abram... oh, I* **know** *this is difficult. You see, I am at the point now where I almost feel foolish doing this. I think, for my protection, he is calling me Nathaniel. But I know he has told Abram that I am really Naomi. So I think there will be a change soon where I will no longer need this type of disguise. I felt very good seeing more women in the other little colony. And so in* *this village I can be safe to be what I am. And I am, you know, growing and getting older and not looking so boyish. So I think I will change.*

It was obvious that more time had passed than I thought. She could have condensed weeks and months in the narrative, especially if they were all alike. Naomi was maturing and taking on the physical characteristics of a young woman.

D: Then this journey has taken longer than a few days. Is that right?
A: *I thought it would be a number of weeks. It changed. Our journeys will change depending on need and what John finds out. So it has been a while, and I guess that's why I feel I am ready to be in one place and be given a responsibility for a while. But I am between my thirteenth and fourteenth year, and I feel I am changing in my body. I will not be able to look like a boy for much longer.*
D: You won't be able to hide it any more.
A: *No. He probably knew I would have to re-emerge as what I was, so this is probably not only a learning place but a safe place to make my transformation.*
D: Yes. Then whenever he comes back and you travel again, it will be as a girl.
A: *And it will be safe and I will feel good. There will probably be more women, so it will be more acceptable.*
D: Was that a surprise, to see more women at the other place?
A: *Yes. I think anyone who is sincere and of truth is accepted, but traditionally most women are brought up like my mother. It appears that there are some who feel as strong about their path as I do about mine.*
D: Yes. The majority of the women aren't even taught anything, are they?
A: *No, it is very rare, very rare.*
D: That's why it would be a surprise to find so many women. I suppose it doesn't matter to the Nazarene, does it?
A: *Oh, he embraces everyone, for he sees differently. He sees people as people. When you live through your heart you are so much more aware of other things that you are not more important if you are a male. You are as important as anyone else. It is not what kind of body you are in. It is what the essence is that shines through that body.*

D: That makes sense to me. Well, are they having a gathering in one of those underground rooms?

A: *Yes. He is welcoming everybody. I think this evening he is trying to get across that he is walking this earth, just as we are, in a body of flesh. And yet what he is or what he can do, all of us are and can do. It is only that we have to open our inner selves to an awareness of acknowledging it. And he believes that once you reemerge through living through the heart and knowing that there is God in you, which is connected to this all-encompassing God, then you will find more understanding. And you will know that you can heal yourself and others, whether it is of the emotions or not. He says you will know that the possibilities are there for all of us.*

D: I suppose many people think he is the only one who can do these things?

A: *Whenever he is questioned about that, he does his best to make people understand that, no, he is made the same as they are. The only difference is that he came to his awareness of human possibilities, and there are no other differences. He dresses like the average man. He wants nothing special. He wants people to know that there is really no difference, and that the laws of God make everybody one. The only important thing is to live through the heart, and to be of service and care for one another.*

D: But of course, he had training, too, to teach him how to be more aware, didn't he?

A: *Yes, but through this training he realized that everything should not be kept so secret, so unavailable to the average person. He believes this was not right. He believes that God's love and laws are for everyone, so this is what he is trying to spread. I guess he is just interpreting what he has learned, so he may teach it to the average person.*

D: Yes, because many of them think these teachings are only for a few people, and not for everyone.

A: *And this has caused much conflict in other levels of society. They feel their power, their hold, is being taken away. Because if the average person discovers that they can think for themselves, and that they can walk their own path and be good and righteous, it will take away their hold.*

D: Then do you think some of the priests know some of these things, but they treat it as sacred knowledge?

A: *I think this is probably the case. I don't know how they interpret it though. Everybody might have access to this knowledge, but the proper interpretation is important.*

D: That's why they don't approve of what he's doing. It's like telling their secrets to everyone. They probably think the average person is not worthy to know many of these things.

A: *That is why he fills you up with such love and contentment, because he tries so hard to get the message through that we all are alike. We are all here to be of service to one another. We should treat each other as we would want to be treated, and be there when somebody is in true need.*

D: Are any of the people asking questions?

A: *Somebody asked, if they spread his teachings and feel that this is to be for everybody and the average person, then how can they protect themselves? How can they truly do this? It is hard to get to that point to dispel the fear.*

D: Yes, a very human emotion. What did he say?

A: *He talked about patience and knowing that if you do not walk in fear, then the eternal light within will grow brighter and brighter, and all those bondages of fear will be released. But we all have to make this discovery for ourselves. And the wise person will proceed with caution and not be afraid of the truth and of reaching out.*

D: But that is a very real fear, because there is danger in what they are trying to do.

A: *Yes. But if you proceed with caution and know you are being asked for this information, then the words slowly penetrate. Once you see that little glow you don't even need words to know that changes are being made. It seems as if people will come to you and ask. And in the asking you will know if you are being of service to someone. That, in itself, is part of the non-verbal communication, showing people you can care. Caring and helping and not demanding anything for it.*

D: But I can understand why they feel that fear. Did anyone else ask a question?

A: *A man also said it was hard for him to understand how he could be his equal. And Jesus goes over to this person and has him feel his hands and his body, to know he is of flesh.*

And to know that if the desire and the intent are there (smiling broadly)... Oh, it's beautiful to watch, because you can see the love coming through his face to this other person. It is as if this other person is mesmerized and doesn't even need words. The Nazarene gives the understanding that no matter what your past has been, if you come to these feelings and revelations at any point in your life, it is alright. It is alright because the **moment** *is of the most importance.*

D: The man probably meant, how could he be equal when Jesus could do all these wondrous things?

A: *And the things that the Nazarene does, he lets him know that he, too, can do them.*

D: That is what is hard to believe. Has he taught these people or the people in your other group how to do the healings?

A: *There have been a few. But it is also a very slow and careful process, because one has to heal oneself first. And if one is given too much, then it does not work the way one had hoped. Then much learning will get confused. It will go backwards or get stopped up. So you have to be very careful, and let them only handle what they are ready for.*

D: Yes, if you give them too much they won't understand it anyway.

A: *And they could be very frustrated. You must also learn that you cannot have expectations. You must learn to have faith. Everything cannot always be translated into words.*

D: Yes, that's true. When he says you must heal yourself first, I wonder what he means by that?

A: *He means that you have to come to the awareness that you* **are** *this being of perfection. You* **are** *this loving God-essence. This is hard to explain, but it is an* **all-** *encompassing feeling of warmth and love and knowing that it is alright to be you. You are perfect the way you are. And through acceptance of this kind of understanding and love, then it can be transferred to others.*

D: Then without that kind of self-love, so to speak, you wouldn't be able to pass on the other teachings, or the healings.

A: *Yes, because the doors will open as you gain your own inner healing. So it is not a quick process... usually.*

D: Have you ever heard of what is called a 'parable'? Have you heard him use that word?

A: (Smiling) *These are found in the written word quite often, I have been told. They are stories that have two meanings, if this is what you talk of?*

D: I think so.

A: *They are written in a way where they will have a* **literal** *meaning, and then there is a* **deeper** *meaning, if you are of the knowledge to see it. And those other meanings hold a truth, a truth that is* **God's** *truth.*

D: You said they were in the written word. You mean in the religious books or what?

A: *This is what I remember from my father's teaching, and the written word of the Holy Books that are read in the Temple. And this is what, when you mentioned 'parable', was my first thought.*

D: Have you ever heard it mentioned in connection with the Nazarene?

A: *I think... I think he has used them, especially when he has talked to the priests and rabbis and government officials, or when he is talking to large groups. At those times he might talk in these 'parables', just to be cautious or keep things peaceful. But he does not use this kind of talk in the smaller groups, because he feels when he is truly wanted and people really want to learn, then he makes it as close and as simple as possible to what the true meaning is.*

D: He doesn't try to be mysterious about it?

A: *No. Only... oh, this is hard to tell. If he has to teach a lesson and somebody has to find their own way... I guess it depends. You see, now I am thinking of other times I remember him speaking. If he is in a large group or if the group is fairly new, then sometimes he will talk this way, but yet he does it only so others might learn. And on the next visit or the next time he meets with them, they will usually discuss it. And by then they would have come up with their own answer. So I guess at times it is a vehicle for teaching.*

D: Then he doesn't tell them what it means. He lets them figure it out for themselves.

A: *Yes. I guess that is the case sometimes.*

D: I thought in some cases he might use it as an example for someone who can't understand any other way.

A: *Yes. I think this is what I was trying to say, too. Because many times they will hear it, and upon reflecting and the passage of time, sometimes it will start their whole re-emergence through opening of the doors. Because they will see it one way and all of a sudden this light will grow, and they will find clarity of understanding. So it is also a learning tool.*

D: I wondered if he sometimes told stories to illustrate a point or to make it easier for the ordinary people to understand?

A: *Sometimes, yes.*

D: Does he talk to the ordinary people on the street, or is it mostly in these groups?

A: *He will not turn anyone away. He will greet ordinary people on the street. If confronted, he will respond. But he has a real feel, he knows when it is right to teach and when he is feeling safe to do so.*

D: That's what I wondered — if he ever had strangers come up to him and want to know what it was all about.

A: *He will answer their questions. He will not turn anyone away.*

D: But the majority of the people he talks to are the ones who know what he's doing.

A: *Yes. Because he feels that by working with **these** people, they will learn the teachings in the truest way and pass them on. Whereas you can't force this knowledge on anyone. That is why he makes these journeys. But as I said, he is constantly teaching, because he will not turn anyone away. He will talk to those people in the street. But it is different from being with those he knows are truly **hungry** and ready for his teachings, and feel this is their path, too. People come to their own reality of this.*

D: Well, these people that he sends out — like at the first town on the lake — to spread the word. Do they just go to the ordinary people, or...?

A: *These people... he sends them in the direction where they are needed. It is not as if he is a commander or a general. These people make their own choices, too. They know they feel a need to be of service. So they are going out on their own journeys and continuing his work, because he can't be everywhere. So they are finding out through their own ways where they are needed. People are linking up. And through messengers these people will make their own journeys to where they can be of most use or are needed the most.*

D: That's what I was trying to understand. They don't go out and recruit or look for new people?

A: *No, because this is not how it happens. Force, he does not work that way.* (Smiling) *He is not* **recruiting***, so the word gets out without any problems. It seems that people are making contact with each other, and it is just spreading.*

D: That's the way it's done. They just tell their friends or whoever they think would be interested.

A: *Or unless they hear of someone in need. They will go out where nobody else would. So this is part of it.*

D: Alright. I was just trying to understand how this all worked. Does anything else happen at that gathering that night?

A: *No. He is mainly answering questions and speaking, and he is finding out where he is needed in the village. He will make contact with various people tomorrow. That seems to be what is happening. I think when his work is done in the village he will be moving on. Whatever it will take to see whoever he needs to see in the village. It probably will not be more than the rest of the day.*

D: Then you will stay at Abram's house. Do you know how long it will be before he comes back?

A: *I am not sure as far as true length of time, but this could be a number of months. I am feeling I need to be in one place and be of service and contribute.*

D: Let's move ahead until he is leaving you there. Did anything happen that was out-of-the-ordinary while he was there in that village?

A: *He did healings, but nothing out-of-the-ordinary* (laugh). *They were just your everyday miracles.*

D: Were they people in the group who were sick, or did they bring people to him, or what?

A: *Oh, they made arrangements for him to visit various homes where he will be accepted, where he is wanted. Not all of them were at the meeting though.*

D: Was there any particular type of illness that he healed?

A: *There was an illness of the... I don't how to say it... the head area. This woman was in horrible pain, as if a vice was being twisted. And there was swelling. You could see a bump on her head, and he released that for her. And she... it was the same. The same golden glow around his head and his heart and his hands. And there was such a softness in his face. But she was able to feel it immediately. And there were people there who saw this happen. It is difficult to believe, but it is a gift of God.*

D: And the swelling went down and the pain stopped?

A: *Yes. She just wanted to* **die**. *She asked to die. But it wasn't her time. And he was able to help her.*

D: Yes, that is a miracle. But, like you said, you are seeing so many of them.

A: (Smiling) *But those other things... he went and saw everybody who needed him, and had another gathering before he was to leave. And he* (smiling) *came over to visit at the house of Abram. And I just...* (deep sigh) *have so much love for him. He placed his hands on my head and my face, and told me that I was to be Naomi, and that I had nothing to fear. That I would always walk with him. And I will learn many valuable lessons, and be of loving service here. He gave me a wonderful hug, and he kissed me on the forehead.* (Sadly, almost crying:) *It is hard to see him leave, but I know this is where I am supposed to be.*

D: But he's going to come back. That's important. He'll come back and get you. He may be going into an area, too, that would be rugged and hard to walk through. He's thinking of your own welfare.

A: (Sniffling) *Yes, maybe.*

D: At least you know you'll be alright there, and you'll be doing what he wants you to do. And he will return. You said you think he will go back towards Jerusalem at that time?

A: *He seems to have to always head back that way at the end of each journey. And so eventually he makes it back to Jerusalem, and the people he has to see there. He will go visit with his family, too.*

D: In Nazareth? Will you be able to go there with him?

A: *I don't know if it will be time, but maybe.*

D: Have you ever heard anyone speak of a man called 'John the Baptist'?

A: *John...?* (Pause)

D: This is a different John. He may be known by a different name.

A: *I think... this man was at the lake. I don't know that he is with him always, but the name is familiar. There was a*

> *man of the name of John when we were at the lake and the little village of Lake Kinnereth. And when we did the cleansing in the water... he said it was for body and spirit. So this might be the man you are speaking of.*

D: This was the man who did it?

A: *Yes. He had a ritual... a symbolic ritual of cleansing. But it wasn't for all of us. There were a few. But I think he was called... I don't know... John of the Water? And it was the cleansing of the spirit ritual.*

D: What kind of ritual was it?

A: *I think this was a ritual of those who had been keeping Jesus' teachings for a while. This was to submerge yourself in the waters, and once you rose up, he said some kind of blessing. And through the symbolic cleansing with the waters of the spirit, it was a ritual of dedication to God and the way of the teachings.*

D: And this is a ritual that's not normally done?

A: *I had heard about it. This was the first time I had seen it.*

D: Are there any other rituals that the Nazarene does with the group?

A: *(Pause) Not with the large group, not with the new group. But he has a manner just of talking and using his hands. When we sit in silent prayer to concentrate on something, you can see and feel a difference. I don't know if this is what you mean. I can't think of anything.*

D: I was thinking that sometimes in the Temple they have rituals and ceremonies.

A: *Oh, like with the candles and the Holy Books and holidays? No, I guess the symbolic water ritual was one of the first. But when I have seen the Nazarene speak, he usually is trying to keep it on a level where there is no separation. So if he is doing something, he tries to make it inclusive of the people there. So he has no ritual, only silent prayer and... the way he asks for guidance from the God of his being.*

D: I suppose ceremonies and rituals would rather put him apart from the normal person. I was curious if he was doing things in the manner that the Temple priests would do. But it's nothing like that.

A: *No. He tries to make his gatherings more like a brotherhood, a fellowship, where no one is higher than another. He sits at the same level and tries to keep it on an*

equal *level.*

D: Alright then. Will it be alright if I come again and speak to you and follow this story? I'm very interested in what happens.

Naomi gave me permission to return and continue pursuing the story of her association with Jesus, so I brought Anna back to her normal conscious waking state. Her life resumed and adjusted to its mundane affairs, while her conscious mind was unsuspecting of the other story that had unfolded so many years ago.

During this session I felt that I, through this unique method of researching history, was allowed a rare privilege of actually attending one of Jesus' gatherings. I felt I was among those present who were learning from the master, and I could see how these teachings were radically different from the orthodox teachings of his day. It was obvious that it took a great deal of courage for these early believers to follow him, because there was much real danger involved. But I was also able to see the charismatic ability he projected in order to put their fears to rest. I was able to feel the quality he possessed that inspired so many people to follow him, so they could learn more about his unusual teachings. Unusual, yes, but they seemed to fill a void in their lives that was not being filled by the traditional teachings of the rabbis of their day.

I was beginning to know the real Jesus.

Chapter Nine

A Vision of Jesus' Death

Several months went by (from March to the end of November) before we could again pursue the story of Naomi's association with Jesus. Anna runs a bed-and-breakfast in her home and during the tourist season she was swamped with customers. So we had to suspend sessions until after this busy time, because there would be no privacy. When we were finally able to arrange a session I used her keyword and we returned to that time period as though there had been no interruption.

When we last talked with Naomi she had been left in a small town to await Jesus' return. I wanted to continue the story from that point. I discovered time had also passed for Naomi.

D: You are returning to the time when you had been left with a friend while the rest of the group continued their journeys. I will count to three and we will be there. 1... 2... 3... we have gone back to the time of Naomi. What are you doing? What do you see?

A: *I see that the Nazarene is coming back into the village. And I am filled with much joy. I hope he will be happy with my progress.*

D: Have you been there long?

A: *It was... an approximate time of three months.*

D: You were staying with a friend of his, weren't you?

A: *I was placed with the family who was to help in my education, and teach me the ways I was seeking. This is the house of Bendavid. And* **oh**, *so much has happened...*

(she became emotional, almost crying) *and... oh, I have changed so very much.*

D: In what way? Can you share it with me?

A: (Sadly) *I... I am overwhelmed with so many emotions, but... I have learned many things from the practical to healing, and to just be of service to my fellow man. I have been taught in the ways of the Nazarene. And I have also been awakened and come very close to knowing love, which I thought was not to be for me. This was not in my plans at all.*

D: That's one thing you were not counting on.

A: (Sniffling) *No.* (She became so emotional she could hardly speak). *I also see so much very clearly now. The emotions are partly from clarity, but just partly from* **pain** (crying). *Because as I look at the Nazarene I see the same radiation of the golden light from the heart center and from around his head. But I know... I can see very clearly of the future. And...* (her voice broke) *it's very difficult to talk about.*

D: Do you mean your future?

A: *I see more of his future.*

D: You mean it is causing you pain to look at him?

A: *Yes, yes.*

D: Did they teach you this ability to see the future while staying there?

A: *No. This is something that I have heard people speak of, but I have not felt the need to tell anyone that I have these visions. I don't have them very often, but I have them. I think, if I be in truth, that seeing him enter the village and seeing the lights I see, I see events happening in my mind. And this does not happen very often, and I have not talked of it. I need to speak to the Nazarene, because I know I can have his true trust and he will listen to me with belief. Whereas in the house of Bendavid I know I am thought of as a family member, but it is still too new. I cannot be forward enough to even talk about these things* (sniffling).

D: Yes, I understand. Are you planning on telling the Nazarene what you see?

A: *Yes, when it is appropriate.*

D: Do you want to share it with me first?

A: *No, I had best wait. It is just that so much has gone on, and until I saw him I did not realize how much I had changed, or the emotions I have been filled with during these past months. As long as I was into the daily routine and learning and growing and doing all that was required of me, it seemed to go quickly. I didn't really have time to sit back and look at it. But it all came rushing to the surface when I saw him, because I knew we would sit down and I would have to tell him* **everything**.

D: Maybe this was one of the reasons why he wanted you to stay there.

A: *Yes. He had to know if I was going to be sure of my commitment. I believe he wanted to give me a chance to change if I chose to do so, which would be accepted with much love and understanding from him.*

D: You said these people that you stayed with are friends of the Nazarene?

A: *Yes. This village is composed of people who believe in his teachings. They believe in truly being of service, and treating each other as we would like to be treated, and walking in the light of God, our Source.*

D: And they were to teach you things while you stayed there?

A: *Yes, I was to learn the philosophy. I was to learn how to care for people and their needs, and to be of service in all ways that I could. I have spent time with the elderly in this village. I have spent time helping the children without families. So I have been educated in all ways of being of service to humankind through* **true** *love and brotherhood.*

D: Where did these people get *their* knowledge? Were they taught by anyone?

A: *These people were taught by the Nazarene. These people have come from various villages and towns, and created their own community. They were the ones who had to meet in secret shelters beneath homes, because it was not accepted that they pursue their beliefs.*

D: Then you have been happy living there?

A: *Yes. I have felt a fulfilment. It is hard to find the words, because the emotions become so overpowering. I have been tested in many ways. But I know that my* **true** *service, my reason for being here at this time, is to learn as much as I can, and to pass this knowledge on through the others I am of service to. And that the love I have discovered is to be one of mutual teaching and growth. That is all I know that can be possible.*

D: You mentioned you had found love, and this was something you were not expecting?

A: *No. I left my parent's house to walk with the Nazarene. If you remember, when I was younger I was allowed to do so because I could be disguised as a boy child. I was not interested in the traditional marriage. I found so much emptiness in the normal accepted ways of life, that my parents and the Nazarene accepted me. They were probably very much surprised when I continued on. And when I could no longer dress as a boy child, I was left in this village where I would be safe. Here I could grow and learn and be sure of my commitment.*

D: But you said he also had other women with him.

A: *Yes. And there were also families who were walking this life of service and truth. There were various women who would volunteer to work with and help ease the pain of the diseased when no one else would walk with him. Therefore women were accepted because they were of healing knowledge, or they were knowledgeable in areas where they could be of service.*

D: I was wondering why he didn't want to take you with him after it became obvious you were a woman.

A: *I think it was the connection to my family... and I was so very young. I was... not thirteen? I was so sure about the path I was to take that I think it surprised all of them. I was so very strong about this that I was going to leave and go off anyway, because it felt so right. After my communion with my God source, all my answers were the same, so I was going to do this. And I think it was very unusual that they found such a serious attitude in one so young, and one that was female, for this is not the Jewish tradition. So I think he had been more cautious, and... it was my age more than anything else, because this was not standard for a woman child of this background.*

D: He is very wise in these things. But you talked about love. Do you mean that you have been attracted to a male?

A: *Yes* (deep sigh). *This is... this is very hard to find words for.* (Sadly again:) *I was so sure that I was to walk this path, and that I was never to know love in that sort of way, because I was strong about my purpose in this life. I never knew that a man could touch me and be spiritual and kind, and treat me as an equal, and really care. I think he became so dear to me because he was part of this household I am in. He helped with my education and he respected me as an equal. I grew to love him... more than a love one would feel for a brother. I did not even know I could have those feelings. And he believes much the same as I do.* (She was almost crying again). *But I cannot see how it could ever be.*

D: What is this young man's name?
A: *His name is Abram* (phonetically, with a heavy accent on the first syllable).
D: Is Bendavid his father?

I had discovered while doing research for *Jesus and the Essenes,* that *"ben"* in front of a name meant "son of".

A: *Yes. So this is Abram Bendavid.*
D: And he lives in the same house. What does he do for a living?
A: *He helps with anything that has to be done in the village, with the repairs on the structures. And he is very knowledgeable in agriculture and irrigation systems.*
D: Then it sounds as if he's very intelligent.
A: *Yes. Everybody has physical responsibilities, plus there is much intellectual growth and spiritual growth that occurs. But everybody is encouraged to learn as much as they can, so they can be physically independent, and everybody can serve a purpose and be of help to one another.*
D: Does Abram feel the same way about you?
A: (Softly) *Yes. But he is so* **willing** *to be patient. He will accept my decisions, because he knows in my heart how dedicated I am. And how, in time, clarity will come and I will truly know my purpose.*
D: Has he mentioned marriage to you?
A: *He has spoken of marriage, but...* (she became very emotional, and tears flowed down her cheeks) *I just feel it's* **impossible.** *Because I can't... I can't be dedicated to both, and it tears me apart.*
D: Maybe this was the reason the Nazarene wanted you to stay there for a while. He wanted you to be sure. But there may be a way of working it out both ways. You never can tell. (I was trying to make her feel better).

A: (Deep sigh) *I don't know.*

I wanted to change the subject since this one was so emotional for her.

D: You said the Nazarene has come back to the village. Are others with him?

A: *Yes, there is a small group with him.*

D: What are *your* plans?

A: *I will do whatever he wishes me to do. I am not sure if my time of education at this village is over, or if I am to stay on. I know I could be of service here, and that I am needed. But in my heart I feel I am supposed to be on more of a pilgrimage, and maybe travel from place to place and be of help and spread the knowledge I have learned. But this is for the Nazarene to tell* **me**.

D: He knows more of the overall plans anyway. Are you going to have some time alone with him?

A: *Yes, this will be necessary.* (She began crying again).

D: You said you wanted to speak with him about the vision you had. Do you plan to do it at that time when you are alone with him? (She was sniffling and sobbing again, and did not answer). Alright. Let's move ahead to that time when you have the opportunity to speak with him in private, and tell me what happens. Did you have time by yourself with him?

A: *Yes.* (She was crying again. It was hard for her to speak).

D: What is it?

A: *It is various feelings. I feel much joy in being with him again. And this feeling is so totally overwhelming that no* **physical** *type of love could ever fill me this way.* (Sadly) *So I* **know** *this love of* **spirit** *and being of service is the only truth there is for me.*

D: They are two opposite things really... or different anyway.

A: (She spoke with sad emotion:) *Not for me. Not for what I'm seeing for me. But I tell him that when I saw him walk into the village, I saw the radiant lights I have seen before. The golden glow around the heart center, and around his head. And I told him that...* (emotionally) *I knew... the pain. I feel the pain. For I know he has walked with truth and love, trying to spread the light, to be an example of what humanity can be. And I know he has been... hurt. I see his heart is very much torn. For I see...* (her voice broke) *his physical departure. I know that he came here to be of service.* (She was crying and it was hard for her to form words)*... But I also see that there are so many that cannot believe. They are so filled with fear that... they will make sure he doesn't live very long.*

D: The way he is to die was part of the vision that you saw? Is that what you mean?

A: (Sadly) *I just saw it happening. I don't know what happens exactly, but I saw him leaving the physical body. And I know that means... that it is his time to go on.*

D: You mean you didn't see how it happened? You just saw that he will die?

A: *Yes, because he came and served his purpose. He walked the land and spread the true philosophy of humankind through God and love and light. He has tried to teach that we are all brothers and sisters. We are all family. And he has done as much as he can do. He knows that there is a minority that will carry on. But his time to ascend is near, because there are deaf ears and dark hearts. His physical presence is meaningless.*

D: What did he say when you told him what you saw? Did he believe you?

A: *When I told him...* (her voice broke again) *it did not come out very easily.* (Sobbing) *I felt I was very confused, because nobody told me things like this would start happening to me.* (Crying) *And I didn't know. I didn't have control. I had trouble feeling this way. And I needed to tell him, because I knew that this dear sweet Nazarene would understand and love me, and know I speak from the heart and from truth.* (Softly) *And he touched my face, and he told me that I need not be afraid, because through his love we would always be connected. He said that my vision was a clear one, and not to fear my visions. But to have respect for them and to see them very clearly and slowly so I don't distort the picture, for these are just God's words coming through my eyes. He said I saw what would truly be his ascending, but that it was his next step. And no matter how it appeared, he was* **done** *with his service on this physical plane. He could go no further, and the handful that accepted the truth of life would endure. But there was so much darkness that he was needed on other levels to* *continue his work.*

D: Then it came as no surprise to him that you had seen this.

A: *No. He listened and understood and accepted what came from my heart. He told me to walk in love and follow the path of the light, and to struggle against fear. There should be no fear, for fear creates the darkness in man. The only truth is the love and light.*

D: (All this emotion was difficult for me also). I am really glad that you told him, so he would know how you felt. Did you also tell him about your love for Abram?

A: *Yes. But when I saw him again I was filled with so much clarity and so much purpose, that I knew what I was supposed to do, even before I said anything. But he understood and he had to allow me to experience those feelings. For mine was a dedication that would continue to grow as long as I accepted my tests and I was honest. He said it was alright to change my path, as long as it was done in love and truth. So he needed me to experience every emotion, and then if I chose not to accept that other path, this was part of my initiation.*

D: So he is still leaving it up to you to decide, isn't he?

A: *I have made the decision. It was made in my own heart and mind before it was ever formed into words, at that moment when we first met and talked. So I have made my decision, and I will walk with him or stay. I only ask to be of service, so that I, too, may ascend and rekindle my connection and growth on that next level.*

D: Does he tell you what his plans are for you?

A: *I was told that I should stay at the village, and that if I have faith and true sensitivity then it will become very clear where I am needed next.*

D: Then at this time he doesn't want you to go with him?

A: *No. I feel very strong. I feel **very** good about my decision. I needed his counsel, for I needed to gain clarity. And I needed to know that my visions and my feelings were of love and light, and not of the darkness. He gave me that assurance that, as long as I seek the truth and be honest, then the fear and darkness will never gain control.*

D: These are very important emotions, very important feelings. I think it's good that you are coming to terms with all of these things. But this will also mean that you will continue to have contact with Abram.

A: *Yes, but it will be much easier now, for I know my mission. I know that much of my purpose is to continue to learn, to heal and ease the pain of the suffering. I will go again to the village of the lepers, of the diseased, and I will have strength, and I will be healthy. For I am meant to help ease the burden and pain of the diseased and the distraught. And I must work with the orphans that desperately need my love. These are purposes of truth and love and light. And these are mine.*

D: Can the followers of the Nazarene go on their own journeys?

A: *We usually go in groups. It would be rare for somebody to travel a distance on their own.*

D: Then you mean that you and some others will go back to that same village of the lepers... without the Nazarene?

A: *I feel there will be very few...* (her voice broke, and she began to cry) *contacts I will have with the Nazarene... in the physical presence. But he promised there will always be contact.*

D: Is that one of the things he wants you to do? To keep returning to these places, even without him, and carry on the work that he started?

A: *He did not say this. This is something that I feel will be mine to do down the road. I feel that is one of the things that will become clear. And, as he said, I will know my path and my purpose as it unfolds. I feel strongly that this will come about.*

D: Do you have any fear of contracting this disease from these people?

A: *No. I have been there before. I feel that if you do not live in fear then you will keep yourself healthy in mind, body and soul. Fear creates all diseases and ailments, whether one is aware of this or not.*

D: That's an interesting idea. Is this what he taught you, that fear creates diseases?

A: *Yes. There were many times in my younger years in my father's village when I would sneak out to attend the closed meetings. And 1 gained this knowledge. This is of his teaching.*

D: Of course, we always think that some diseases can't be avoided. He doesn't believe this way?

A: *No. I say, though, that one must be a believer in the*

Source within one's being. That is one's God-center, that is one's heart center. If one lives without fear, one has placed a great healing protection throughout one's physical being and other layers of protection around the human person. If you let fear or darkness enter your being, you open up a space that will allow ailments to grow. One can control any disease of the mind or body.

D: Do you think this is one of the ways he is able to heal people?

A: *Yes, for those people that have come to him and asked to be healed have created a healing* **path** *in their own hearts and minds. It is just connecting with* **his** *energy, because they have already set up their belief of trust. Then they have eliminated the fear and the darkness, which enables them to accept the healing. So even though the Nazarene has the power to heal, the person who is ailing has to have within himself his own power to release his fears and the disease of his flesh. Or if they are not meant to be healed or continue on with this life, they will find it a very easy transition to ascend in true peace and love, and they will go on to the next existence.*

D: Can he heal someone that doesn't want to be healed, or if they don't know about it?

A: *I search my past and* (chuckle) *I see that he will heal the ailing bird, the ailing animal. He is very much aware of those people who are not of truth and are testing him, for he exposes them. But the people who come in truth, he can and will heal, unless there is some reason holding back the healing. He will let them know this.*

D: Has it happened that people have tried to test him?

A: *Oh, yes, he has been tested many times, on many occasions. Even when he went underground there were infiltrators every now and then, but he is of such purity and sensitivity that the tests are very obvious to him.*

D: Could you give me an example of one that you were a witness to?

A: *There was a soldier, I remember, in Jerusalem, and he paid a beggar to lie about a healing. I saw the Nazarene pick out this fraud and he even exposed the soldier.*

D: What would the soldier have gained from something like that?

A: *The soldier wanted to turn the people against him. The people who were just beginning to listen to him. For the Romans were very threatened by his...* (she couldn't find the word).

D: Abilities?

A: *Abilities, but the populace was beginning to listen.*

D: Then the soldier paid the beggar... to pretend he had been healed or what?

A: *To say that he had been healed, but an infection had come back. He had a festering wound. That is what I remember. He stood up before the crowd and showed this festering wound, which he told them had been healed by this man they called 'Jesus'. And this is what had happened to the wound. But the crowd was told the whole story by the Nazarene, and he even pointed out the soldier. The crowd turned on the soldier and started throwing stones, but this upset the Nazarene very much. And there was another incident where a blind man was brought to him, and Jesus was not able to cure him. He was able to point out to the man, the crowds, and the people who were trying to cause problems, the reasons why this man would not regain his sight.*

D: What were the reasons?

A: *There were things he had done in his life, but also he was given blindness as a teacher. He was given blindness so he would turn inward, and heal the darkness and the fear within and let the light come through so he could live in truth. For sight does not give one clear vision. This man had done some horrendous things in his earlier years, and the blindness was caused in an accident. So he was spared his life. But this man, who was going to try to make the Nazarene look like a fraud, was filled with such love and understanding that he accepted his blindness. There was something **within** him that was healed, to cause him to accept his life and to be of service.*

D: How does the crowd react at these times when he can't heal someone? Do they become angry if he can't *always* do these things?

A: *If a healing cannot take place, there is a reason given. And I would say it is so acceptable that it really cannot be questioned, because it is filled with such truth. But since the Romans and the Jews of the Temple live in such fear of him, he has chosen to be of service in these various*

villages where he is accepted and needed and wanted.
D: Then he tries to stay away from Jerusalem? Is that what you mean?
A: *Yes, because it hinders his progress.*
D: Have you ever seen him do anything else besides the healings, that was different or out-of-the-ordinary?

I was thinking of other miracles mentioned in the Bible. She paused as though thinking.

D: Or if you have not seen it personally, have you heard stories of things he had done that the ordinary person couldn't do?
A: *I have seen the illuminations from his hands. I have seen him heal people's very* **souls***, their hearts. I have... I have seen him survive things that people might not normally survive.*
D: Do you have any example of something like that?
A: (Deep sigh) *I know he was taken by the Roman soldiers beneath the courts and tortured. I know he was placed in a cart that was not big enough for a man to survive in. And he was thrown over the ravine... and he survived. I hesitate in talking about this, because since those times he has been protected in various villages. I have seen him survive physical things, but the miracles have been in the healing, in the food, in finding enough to care for people's needs.*
D: Why did the soldiers do that to him?
A: *They were trying to find various ways to destroy him, because he was gaining too much power. He was beginning to gain many followers who were questioning the Roman laws and the equality and fairness of life under them. They were gaining strength, and talking of rebelling, for this is not how you treat your fellow man. So the soldiers were trying to destroy the Nazarene and make it appear that others had done it.*
D: Did they do this without any authority?
A: *They had authority. They had their king's authority.* (Sadly:) *But they will succeed. They will find enough dark people, and they will succeed.*
D: But at that time, did they arrest him? You said they tortured him. I'm curious about what happened.
A: (As though I had brought her attention back to the other

story. She had been thinking of the future event). *Oh, yes. They took him without causing a scene. It appeared to be a friendly ploy, but it was a matter of kidnap. There are mazes and cellars under the courts. And they took him there and threatened him and tortured him. They thought this would be enough. When they found out he would not succumb, then they started infiltrating the streets, and getting anyone they could find to do their deeds. There are many who can be paid off. Many poor Roman followers were very eager to do the bidding of the soldiers.*

D: Then you said after they tortured him they put him in a small cart?

A: *Yes, a crate, a box. And they rolled him off a ravine feeling surely this would kill him. And it did not. So now they continue to infiltrate the streets and pay people to bring down his reputation, to make him seem what he is not. For there are many of those who can be bought off and turn in their own kind, too. And they will, of course, blame it on the people of the Temple. The Nazarene chose to walk his own path because he found those within the Temple to be as cruel and manipulative as within the Roman courts. So...*

D: I would think that after he survived going off into the ravine, that the Romans would have reacted differently.

A: *The Romans were filled with* **more** *fear, because they know these private villages are forming. His followers are growing. Every time he has a healing, every time something happens, or a person who had a dark personality has changed —just like the blind man — it creates more believers. If he knows someone from the Romans is going to try to mistreat him, he will confront them with this. He is made aware of who has turned on him. He went — even though he was aware of the kidnap — because he thought he might be able to heal within the hierarchy of the government. So he has chosen to allow his physical being to go through what it must for his own lessons on this earth.*

D: He did that for a reason then, because he knew it was going to happen. I would think that after seeing him survive, the Romans would realize he wasn't an ordinary human being.

A: *This was more apparent to them, so they sped up their intervention on the streets. They knew that unless they turned the masses against him they would not survive — they would not retain their power. So they lived in more fear after he survived.*

D: That is why he doesn't want to return to Jerusalem any time soon.

A: *Yes. But he will return because there are people there that need him. He knows he must carry out his plans and his mission, so he will go back.*

D: Maybe this was why he didn't want to take you back to Jerusalem.

A: *After I told him of my vision and he told me of the truth and clarity in it, he also told me there was no need to walk with him. My mission was to stay at the village where I was needed and could be of service. I could grow here, and then my next path would become clear to me. But I know* **why** *he does not want me to come. He does not want me to be there. There is no reason to go, for we both know what will happen.*

D: I thought maybe he was afraid to take you back into the city, because they would be looking for him.

A: *Yes, but there is no need for me to go.*

Amazingly, in this session Anna supplied missing parts of a story that she consciously didn't even know. When Jesus decided to return to Jerusalem on Palm Sunday, his disciples feared for his safety, but the Bible never makes it clear why. Now it was obvious why they didn't want him to return. He had already been exposed to torture and near-death several times.

He was safe if he stayed in the Nazareth area because that was Philip's (Herod Antipas' brother) domain, and he was beyond the power of the Jerusalem authorities. From Capernaum he could also easily avoid Herod Antipas. The Romans did not normally send their troops that far away from their stronghold in Jerusalem. He could also find privacy in these smaller towns, if he desired it for himself and his disciples. He could be more open in his teachings in these communities, away from the larger cities. But in some areas, such as the meetings in the caves around the Sea of Galilee, he knew he had to be more careful, because of the possible presence of spies.

This must have been John's job to speak with the organizers

of the meetings, to know which areas would pose a danger, in which case hidden meeting places would have to be arranged. Jesus did not go blindly into these areas. He had information concerning the group's safety before John would allow him to enter. He was safe in the village of the lepers because this was a place to be shunned, and only selfless devoted people like his group would have the courage and the caring to go there. In such places he had no worry about being overheard by spies planted by Rome. He could relax and live a seemingly normal life. This was probably why he sought out these isolated towns.

In Jerusalem there were many diverse nationalities and religions, and many had difficulty understanding Jesus' teachings. Even among the Jews there was a variety of spiritual and mental outlooks, even heathen. Among all these were nationalists, often natives of Galilee, to whom God and people, God and Jerusalem, God and the Temple, were inseparable objects. They burned with indignation over everything which was not in accord with this unity. Against this background, Jesus was perceived as not national enough for the nationalists, too old-fashioned for the Sadducees, too modern and liberal for the Pharisees, and too strict for the ordinary people of the street. He had a difficult time trying to be all things to all people.

In Jesus' time the only education was "education in religion". They were taught that the Law of Moses was the most important teaching and the only thing they were expected to base their life and their thinking on. Jews were not taught to think for themselves, or to question the rabbis or the priests. In Jerusalem Jesus was viewed with suspicion, because he was asking people to go against the only teaching they had ever been exposed to. He was asking them to listen to a totally different way of thinking, and many were incapable of doing so. It was much easier to present his new and radical ideas to those in the outlying towns who were open to listening to ideas that were contrary to their upbringing.

It was not easy for people to listen and accept concepts that were totally opposite to everything they had been taught all their life. Many considered him a dangerous radical, and his teachings the ramblings of a madman. Historians claim that Jesus' famous Sermon on the Mount could never have been preached in the Jerusalem area, because that city was a hot-bed of tradition. The sermon presented the opportunity to the listeners to look beyond tradition and the exact letter of the Law, to a new and enlarged application of old sayings and truths. Such a state of mind would not have generally been found in Judaea at that time, but was exactly what could be expected in the region of Capernaum.

Jesus had turned the rabbis, priests and traditional Jews against him because he thought the priests in the Temple concentrated too much on rituals and the performance of ceremonies. They did not look at the problems and concerns of the people. Jesus saw that there was a greater conflict than the one between Rome's tyranny and the Jewish belief that they were the chosen people of God.

The people in Palestine had real cause to be afraid of the Romans. During Jesus' lifetime, at the beginning of the reign of Herod Antipas, some Jews tried a rebellion. It was put down by the superior strength of the Romans, and two thousand Jews were crucified as punishment. The people lived with the oppression of a harsh ruler, but their hope for a redeemer, a Messiah, a savior, to lead them out of it, showed that they were desiring an overthrow of the existing government and a return of their lost freedoms.

The Zealots used these emotions to fuel their cause. They thought that Jesus would be the new king in the literal sense, and that he would side with them in a real war to free the country. His mild ways and talk of love angered them, because they expected violence to be the answer. Judas Iscariot is now recognized as probably belonging to the Zealots. This was one of the reasons behind his betrayal of Christ: he thought he could force Jesus into a situation where he would have to fight, and the rest of the people would join him. The Romans were very aware of the volatile situation in Jerusalem. and the possible danger presented by anyone who might appear as a leader.

When Jesus entered the city on Palm Sunday, exalted by the cheering throng, the Romans knew they would have to get rid of him by any means. His popularity had grown to a threat that menaced them. The people were acknowledging him as the long awaited Messiah who would lead them from bondage and slavery to the Romans. He was the man who would lift the yoke. The authorities saw that this man Jesus could be the one to stir the people into rebellion. This gentle man could no longer be tolerated. He would have to be eliminated.

My research revealed that the underground area of Jerusalem is riddled with old passageways and secret chambers. These areas, and sections of two walls, are the only parts that remain of the original Biblical city. There were many chambers beneath the site of the Temple. Some of these were used by Roman soldiers to provide secret access from their fortress at the corner of the Temple wall to other areas, as a means of defense. It is logical to assume this was the area Naomi refers to, where Jesus was taken to be questioned and tortured, in the hope he would be intimidated into giving up his radical teachings.

The ravine into which Naomi said he was thrown was mentioned in all the historical data referring to the ancient city. At the time of Jesus the city was divided by a ravine called the Tyropoeon Valley, spanned by a bridge. On the east side of the enormously high Temple wall lay the Kedron ravine or Kedron Valley, which was also spanned by a bridge from the Mount of Olives. Josephus said this valley was so deep you could not see the bottom when looking down from this wall. According to the historical research Jesus' brother James was murdered there, when he was thrown from the wall down into the ravine. This occurred in the turbulent time following Jesus' death on the cross. These valleys no longer exist.

If Jesus was able to survive the torture and death attempts of the Romans, then it should be obvious that he could have escaped being arrested and crucified. He died only because he chose to do so. As Jesus says in the Bible, (*John* 10:17-18) "I lay down my life, that I might take it again. No man taketh it from me, but I lay it down of myself. I have power to lay it down, and I have power to take it again." If he had not decided it was his time to ascend, and it was not fitting into the pattern of his life, then he would not have allowed the Romans to kill him. It appears from this story that he had great control over his body, even to the extent that he could survive what would have killed others who were not so developed. He knew and understood his mission to the point that he could control the time and method of his death.

Chapter Ten

Naomi's Story of the Crucifixion

Another month went by and it was almost Christmas 1987 before we could have another session. I rarely have sessions during the winter months because of the possibility of bad weather and heavy snows which can occur in Arkansas in winter. I don't like the idea of being stranded on our mountain roads after dark. These are the times of hibernation in our Ozark mountain country, but I did desire to complete Anna's story of Naomi's association with Jesus. At this time I was writing the first two Nostradamus books, and my attention was completely absorbed with that intense and complicated information.

It soon became obvious that it didn't matter how much time elapsed between the sessions. Anna was able to pick up the story at the exact point each time, as though there had been no interruption. In the meantime she continued with her own life, and said she did not even think about the regression story. This was more evidence to me that it was not being fantasized, because there was not an overwhelming compulsion to continue with the sessions. They were almost incidental to her busy life. Her attention was only focused on it when we had a session. When Anna awoke she would display confusion and disbelief, but after I went home her attention focused once again on her daily routine. Naomi would recede back into the recesses of her subconscious, and into the recesses of time.

As the story progressed it looked as though Naomi would not be present in Jerusalem when Jesus was crucified because he had told her to stay in the village. I really believe she would not have wanted to be present anyway. It would have been extremely difficult and heart-wrenching for anyone who had been closely associated with him to watch such a horrible spectacle. She appeared to be as sensitive and caring as real-life Anna is now, and she couldn't have observed such a scene. But I thought she would surely hear the news and the different tales and versions of what happened. We could learn much from these accounts. I used Anna's keyword and counted her back through time.

D: Let's go back to the time when Naomi was living at the house of Bendavid, and Jesus had just been speaking with her. Let's go back to that time. What are you doing? What do you see?

A: *I am leaning against a tree. I have been out walking. And I have been thinking. I seem to have a clearer picture of my future.*

D: Can you share it with me?

A: (Sadly, but not emotionally as before, with calm resolution:) *I know I am meant to walk the pilgrimages of the Nazarene, and to be of service in the villages and the areas where people need help. And I know I am to go back to the leper colonies and be of service. I know my visions have been filled with truth. And I know that my time with the Nazarene is drawing to an end.*

D: What do you mean?

A: *I know that he will not be with us physically for much longer.*

D: Is this because of the vision that you had?

A: *Yes. And when we talked he told me I saw the truth. He said that his mission and purpose for walking among the people is coming to a close, because his purpose is almost at an end in his physical body.*

D: Have you decided what you are going to do?

A: *I will stay in this village as long as I am needed. And then I will travel with the smaller groups that do service for*

*those in areas where most people will not go. I want to be
of service where people are needed the most, and there is
a group that does the pilgrimage year round. So I believe
this is my destiny.*

D: Has the Nazarene left yet?

A: *He will leave in the morning.*

D: Do you know where he's going?

A: *I believe he's going to make one more pilgrimage. And
then he will be going towards Jerusalem. He has people to
meet with.*

D: What sort of people? Do you know?

A: *I know he has to see some of his followers. For he also
knows that those who wish to do him harm will come for
him soon. And he must prepare himself.*

D: Did he tell you anything about what he knows?

A: *No, not with clarity. He just told me what I saw was truth,
and that we would be in contact, but not in our physical
bodies any more.*

D: I was wondering if you were planning to go with him in
the morning.

A: *No, he does not wish me to walk with him. He wishes me
to stay in this village right now. Then he feels that my
service in a pilgrimage is very important. He feels that I
will serve the cause and the spirit better by staying safe
and healthy where I can.*

D: You always want to do what he wants you to.

A: *Yes, sometimes it is difficult. I know that I truly am needed
here. I feel very old at times. I feel at peace with my
decision. But I am so clear with my visions that I know
what is going to happen. And this is the plan of God, so I
accept it with strength.*

D: Yes, because if he also knows what's going to happen, he
could avoid it if he wanted to.

A: *But he was sent here for a purpose, such as we all are.
And his purpose has been served. So in ascending he will
continue to grow, and do far more good than remaining in
the physical body at present. So he does this for his own
growth in spirit.*

D: Do you have any desire to return to Jerusalem to see your
parents?

A: *I do, but this will come later.*

D: Alright. Let's move ahead to the morning when he is

getting ready to leave. Did you see him before he left?

A: (Sadly, almost crying) *Yes. There are a few people that are leaving with him.* (Softly, almost inaudible:) *And... I... I am just having some trouble,* (she began to cry) *because I know.. I know his path is going to be filled with* **pain** *and* **accusations.** *And yet I look at him, and his eyes are so kind and loving. I see the golden glow from his heart center and around his head.* (Her voice broke). *And I can't begin to find the words. It is hard to see him leave this time.*

This emotion was contagious. It was difficult to interrupt, yet it was important to move the story forward.

D: But they are going on their pilgrimage, you said?

A: *Yes... and this will be his last.*

D: Did he say goodbye to you?

A: (Softly) *Yes. He put his hands on my face and looked at me and... wished me to continue to walk while being led by my heart and my spirit. And that is the truth* (Crying).

D: I know you have felt very close to him, that's why it's emotional for you. But it's very wonderful to have had contact with a person like that. Alright. Let's leave that scene, and move ahead. I want you to move to the next time that you see him and have contact with him, if there is a next time.

I did not think there would be a next time, since she was so certain she would not see him again before he died, but I thought we should see. I guess I was still hoping there was a way to get her to Jerusalem in time to witness the crucifixion and give an eyewitness account.

D: Let's move ahead in time till the next time that you meet with him.

When I finished the sentence she gave an outburst of emotion and tears. I thought maybe she was seeing his death.

D: It will be alright. If it bothers you too much you can always watch it as an observer. What's happening?

A: (Tearfully) *I am... it 's... oooh!*

D: What is it?

A: *I am on the road, and I am walking into the village of the lepers. And he has been gone. I mean, he has had his physical death. But yet there he is... I see him! I see him on the road!*

D: Can you tell me what he looks like?

A: (Crying) *He looks the* **same**. *Except he is in a fresh robe, but he looks the* **same**.

D: As though he was physical, you mean? Has he been gone very long?

A: *Oh, it feels like a number of months.*

D: What is happening?

A: (She was almost overcome with emotion) *He... he is not talking with his mouth, but with his mind. He wanted me to know that he is with me always, and that he loves me. And that he takes pride that I have had the strength to continue to be of service. And to not fear for myself, but to help those who cannot help themselves. This is why he picked this time to make himself clear to me.*

D: Are you alone on that road when you see him?

A: *Yes. I took a break from the village. I do this. I go for walks. And it is safe to do this. I go for short walks when I need to think or just get away by myself for a while.*

D: Then no one else saw him. Does he communicate with you very long?

A: *No, but he lets me know that he is with me and he will stay with me and appear to me. And that he is in a better place, where he has things to do, where he is needed* (smiling).

D: Then did he just walk away or what?

A: (Softly) *He seems to have disappeared. I am alone again on the road.*

D: You must have heard the stories of what happened to him. Can you tell me? (Pause) You weren't there, were you?

A: (Still emotional) *No. But there were the Roman soldiers, from what I understand, and he was arrested. And they found him guilty* (almost inaudible) *and put him to... death.*

I had to ask questions as though I was ignorant of the Biblical story, in order to not influence her, and to obtain her unbiased version.

D: Wasn't there anything his friends could do?

A: *They didn't have enough strength. You can't fight the Roman soldiers unless you have more strength, more power than they do.*

D: I didn't think they could just put someone to death without a reason.

A: *They said he was being blasphemous against the Roman... the government. Also some of the religious leaders felt he was being blasphemous against God and their teachings. They felt they could not let this man live, who was spreading these types of things against the government, and against the Temple. And they felt he was... they felt...* (her voice broke).

D: What?

A: (She regained composure) *They felt what he was saying was not filled with any truth, and that he had been lying to everyone. They said he could not perform miracles. They tried to force him to perform miracles. And he could not. And then there was rioting. His followers, his handful of followers were fighting the soldiers in the street. And there were people trampled and dying.*

D: Do you mean his followers were fighting with the Romans over what they were saying?

A: *His followers were trying to protect him.*

D: To keep him from being arrested, you mean?

A: *Yes, and there weren't enough of them.*

D: Then some of them were dying on the streets?

A: *Yes. The soldiers started fighting, and then the town went crazy. People were being trampled and the soldiers were just going after anybody.*

D: You said they tried to make him perform miracles and he couldn't. Do you think he couldn't or he just wouldn't?

A: *I think...* (firmly) *I think they would have found a way to kill him, no matter what. I think he knew that miracles can happen for anyone. But if they don't believe that they can be healed or things can be changed, it will not happen. He couldn't make a blind man see if the blind man didn't want to see. Or if there is something else that the blind man was supposed to be doing.*

D: I guess it was a test they were giving him.

A: *A test that was meant for him to fail, and he knew it. He made that trip knowing the outcome. He* **knew** *what was* *going to happen. They would not have made a test that he could have survived. They felt too threatened.*

D: It would be hard to perform miracles in that kind of atmosphere anyway.

A: *Yes. And also he was not walking among the people for this purpose. So they put him on a... it was a trial but it was a mockery. And then they planned his... death.*

D: Do you know how he was killed? (Naomi uttered a deep sigh). I know this is disturbing for you to answer these questions, but I just want to know what you were told.

A: *Well, they kill people... they make wooden crosses.* ('Crosses' seemed to be an unfamiliar word to Naomi). *This is how they put people to death... in the worst way in these times. They put up these wooden crosses and they nail people there. And they let them die. They kill people,* **many** *people, this way. Especially those they want to make an example for others. They want to make sure they can control the masses by fear.*

D: That sounds like an awful way to do it. Have you heard any other stories of what happened at that time?

A: *I have heard many stories. I don't know what is really true. But some people say that they saw him die up on that cross, and yet they saw him appear to them the following evening or the next day. And then I have also heard that they couldn't find his body. I have heard many things.*

D: Did you talk to anyone who was actually there when he died?

A: *Yes. I talked to people who saw him up on the cross.*

D: Did they tell you anything that happened while he was dying?

A: *They said that somehow he was able to control the pain.*

D: That is wonderful. Then you know he didn't suffer.

A: *I heard someone say they saw the same kind of glow that I saw from his heart center and from his head. They saw the same golden lights. They also saw that when he was taken down from the wooden hanging, that there was a calmness over his face.* (Reflective pause) *But I have heard that people saw him appear afterwards.*

D: Was he hanging there long? I've heard it takes a long time to die that way.

A: *I don't remember in time. I don't remember...*

D: But he was able to control the pain.

A: *Yes. I heard that from a number of people. They were surprised at how calm he was. It was as if he was not there.* (Pause) *By the morning he was... I know they had him down by early dawn.*

This same statement, about Jesus not suffering and apparently not feeling pain, was reported in *Jesus and the Essenes.* It was as though he removed himself, maybe by going out of his body. However he did it, he was advanced enough to know how to separate himself from what his body was experiencing. It is also reported that he died in a vastly shorter time than crucifixion normally takes. So he apparently had complete control over his physical body.

D: You said you heard people say they couldn't find his body?
A: *That's what I have heard.*
D: What did you hear about that?
A: *I heard they had put his body to rest and covered it over. And that there were soldiers guarding.*
D: Why were the soldiers there?
A: *I think the Romans were very much afraid of his followers and of the reputation he had. They were getting worried. So, I guess they thought he was a prisoner of the government.*
D: Even after he died?
A: *Yes. I think they were filled with so much fear because he had gained so much control. That is why they could not let him live any longer. I heard that the followers were going to come and get the body.*
D: That's why they had soldiers there?
A: *Yes. But I heard that when they went to take the cover off, the body was not there. This is what I have heard* (chuckling, as though it was absurd). *I don't know. The soldiers went to check. I think the followers and the family finally were allowed to see the body. And I think that eventually the government might have given the body to the family. But they went to check, and they said the body was gone. I don't know what might have really happened. They could have drugged the soldiers or made them drunk. The followers could have taken the body. They might have done many things to make it appear that the body had*

disappeared on its own.

D: It's hard to believe, isn't it?

A: *Yes. There are many stories being heard. And if you were not there... they have grown. The stories grow by the time they reach you. But I know that the government and the Temple were fearful of the following and the power, and hearing of the miracles and the healings that took place. They were feeling threatened, so they would have eventually found a way to kill him.*

D: Yes, it sounds as if they saw him as a threat. But we know he never did anything that would have hurt anyone. You said you also heard stories that he appeared to people? Do you mean in the way he appeared to you on the road?

A: *I heard that he started appearing right in Jerusalem.*

D: Do you know who he appeared to?

A: *No. Different groups of people. I just heard that he started appearing in a few places.*

D: I wonder if he looked as he did when you saw him, or if he was like a spirit. Did they say they recognized him?

A: *They say that he appeared and then he was gone. But that he looked the same. They recognized him.*

D: Did anyone say if he spoke to them or not?

A: (Pause) *One group said they heard him say they were forgiven. I have not heard what the others have said, but he hasn't talked each time. Sometimes he just appears.*

D: Do you know if he appeared to any of his followers, besides you?

A: *Yes. I heard that he appeared to them... and said that he forgave all, and that they should find the strength to live the truth and to continue the teaching of God.*

D: What do you think he meant by 'he forgave *them*'? His followers?

A: *Because there was someone — there was actually more than one. He was betrayed. The Romans had to know how to trick him in front of the public.*

D: What is the story you've heard about that?

A: *The Romans found followers that they could pay off through power or wealth.*

D: I would not have thought any of his followers would do that.

A: *There were many people who claimed to be followers, but men can be readily tempted when it comes to making their own personal life easier. And not many regret it later.*

D: I can't see how anyone who had been close to him and walked with him could betray him.

A: *The Romans knew which ones to go to.*

D: How did they betray him?

A: *They gave the Romans information that would serve to set up a plan of trickery, to be able to accuse him, as well as to be able to have him fail. They came up with the idea of presenting a challenge that they knew would fail. They would have somebody not be healed and a miracle not happen. They knew how to make it appear before the public that the Nazarene was not real. That this man was against the people. There was a huge crowd gathered, and the Roman soldiers started to question the Nazarene in public and to accuse him and make him seem like a fool. And there was a large crowd. When he could not do what they asked, then they yelled, 'He has not done any of the things that people say he has. He is some sort of a... demon'. They turned the crowd into a mob. It was a riot.*

D: But you told me one time that they had tried these kinds of tests before, and Jesus was able to expose them. Why didn't he do it this time?

A: *He knew this was his time. This was how he was supposed to ascend. He knew this when he had his own turning on him. He knew that the people, the masses, were not ready for his ways of truth and life. He knew there was a small group of people that would continue his work. But he knew this was far too brutal and primitive a world, so he had served his purpose. He had, at this time, done what he could do. And it was his time to work from a different area.*

D: Did you hear any other stories of people seeing him after he died?

A: *Yes. As the months went on I started hearing that he had appeared in some of the smaller villages that he used to go to, where his following was. And... I hear these things but I... they say that he has performed healings and miracles. I know that people have probably seen him, but I wonder if amongst his followers, if they are living through their heart and living the truth, if they are probably doing their own healings. And feeling that, because they have seen him, he has performed the miracles. But I think in seeing him it has given them strength and faith to continue.*

D: That could be. Well, what happened to the followers?

A: *They live in much fear. The ones in the city, where they feel they are safe, continue with their basement meetings. And the ones in the outer villages are going on with their lives. They are still his followers, but they can be his followers and the government does not have to know. And then the people on the pilgrimages... well, nobody cares about those people that they help anyway. So they are reasonably safe.*

D: The Romans don't see them as a threat.

A: *No. The government does not care about the lepers or the villages that are so poor. They are not going to help. And nobody wants to minister to the sick. They are afraid of the diseases. So we are safe.*

D: They probably think that without a leader the others won't do anything anyway.

A: *That's true. So they can keep it subtle and below the surface, and still continue to teach and live the truth the best way they can.*

D: I thank you for telling me the stories you have heard. At least you know that *you* saw him, so you know that part is true.

A: *Yes, and I feel him. I mean, I am filled up. I know he is with me.*

D: Have you returned to Jerusalem to see your parents yet?

A: (Sigh) *I will be doing that on my next pilgrimage towards that area.*

D: They're probably wondering what happened?

A: *I have tried to send messages to them by way of people going in that direction. So I hope they have received them.*

D: If you have a chance to talk to them, they may know more of the facts of what happened, because they were in the same city. Alright, let's leave that scene. And let's move ahead to the next time that you go to Jerusalem to see your parents. Let's move to that time. Did you ever return to Jerusalem?

A: *Yes.*

D: I suppose it was probably emotional after not seeing them for so long.

A: *Yes, They are... oh, I noticed... well, I'm so much older. So*

I noticed the age, but I also noticed the sadness. There is a **calm** *sadness.*

D: What caused that, do you know?

A: *Just the upheaval in the government, and being pulled in so many directions. It has been very difficult for them. They were believers in what the Nazarene said, but they were not true followers. They held onto some of their traditional beliefs, yet they could not quite believe in the Temple laws because of the cruelty and injustice. So they do the best they can just to survive day-to-day.*

D: But didn't you say your father was the Nazarene's brother?

A: *He was a half-brother, but he varied in some of his beliefs. I think after what they went through with how he died, and knowing that he was accused of things that were not true, they lost part of their heart. They are just making motions, and going through life right now, it seems.*

D: Yes, I can understand that. Can you ask them if they were there when he died?

She spoke slowly as though she might have asked them, they were answering, and she was repeating.

A: (Sadly) *They saw him up on the cross. And they prayed. My father said there was a time when he looked up, and their eyes met. He said he felt... he felt a warmth and a love.* (Emotionally) *And it was not of this world, he said.*

D: Can you ask him if anything unusual or out-of-the-ordinary happened? (Her facial expression showed emotion). What?

A: *Well...* (deep sigh) *he said... and it is as if I am seeing it through my father's eyes. He said that when they took him down he saw a vision of his brother in a clean robe, as if in another body...* (crying) *as if the physical body went one way, and this other body that appeared as he knew it when it was whole and healthy, went another way. He saw the same thing I saw on the road.* (Tearfully) *And he described the same thing and the same feeling.*

D: Ask him if he heard the tales that the body had disappeared? Does he know anything about that?

A: *Yes. He said that the following morning they were going to get his body. And they opened the granite lid, and he said the body was gone.*

D: He saw that it was gone?

A: *Yes, but he really doesn't know how to explain it. Because, like me, he said many things could have happened, between the soldiers and some of his closer followers and the religious people. My father feels, after what he had seen at the cross, that the physical body had no meaning. But he said there was no* **body**.

D: Was anyone else with your father when he went there?

A: *He said some of the followers that walked with the Nazarene. There were maybe a dozen of them.*

D: What did the soldiers think when the body was gone?

A: *At first the soldiers were in shock. Then they became angry, because they knew they would be held responsible for whatever happened. But there was definite shock, because they had no idea how the body disappeared.*

D: Then it would seem that they didn't have anything to do with it.

A: *No. I believe there are various kinds of herbs or spices you can mix in food or drink, and make people sleep. So I don't know. There were many ways this could have occurred. The soldiers have no memory of anything, so they say.*

D: Yes, that sounds possible. Could someone have slipped by them then and got to the body?

A: *I think it might have happened.*

D: The place where he was wasn't sealed or anything?

A: *He was placed in a tomb, and then this tomb was guarded by the soldiers. So it would have taken some planning to do this, if the body did not disappear on its own.*

D: Is that possible, do you think?

A: *I do not think so.*

D: That would be very strange.

A: *Yes. I don't know what the government, the followers, the religious leaders, or whoever might have done this, were planning.*

D: Yes. But anyway, the body was gone. I thought the tomb might have been sealed so no one could get in.

A: *It was supposed to be that way. But... it would have taken more than two people to get that top off the tomb. It was heavy. So something was planned.*

D: Are you going to stay with your parents very long?

A: *No, just a short visit. Then I have places to go, people to care for.*

D: Are you by yourself?

A: *No, there are other followers that came into Jerusalem. I don't go on the road by myself. It is a small group usually.*

D: Well, I know your parents are glad to see you and to visit with you.

A: *Yes. It is good seeing them. But this place is very foreign to me.*

D: It must seem like a long time since you left there.

A: *Yes. And the whole atmosphere of this area does not feel right to me.*

D: I suppose there are many changes since you left. *You* have changed in many ways since you left your parents' house.

A: *Yes.* (Chuckle) *Lifetimes.*

D: Many changes. Alright. Let's leave that scene, and I want you to move ahead one more time to an important day in your life that occurred after that time. An important day when something that you consider to be important is happening. I will count to three and we will be there. 1... 2... 3... it's an important day in your life. A day that you consider to be important. What are you doing? What do you see?

A: *I am in a village. And I am quite a bit older.* (Her voice definitely sounded older). *But we have been very successful in evolving a community based on the truth and the teachings of the Nazarene and of God. I know this group will go on to teach others, and that it will never die. And that* **someday** *this hope he had for humanity will evolve into what he wanted it to be. So I guess this day is important mainly because I know my own time is coming nearer. And I can ascend with a full heart knowing that I have taught many people, and that they are true. They will continue to teach others and grow. I have been with this family of mine now for many years in this community. And we are safe. We are safe from the government and the religion. We can still go off on pilgrimages and be of service. And yet we are growing and we have strength.*

D: Did anyone give your village a name?

A: *Yes. We have called it Bethsharon.* (Phonetic. Accent on the last syllable).

My Jewish consultant said Beth in front of a place name meant "house" (an example is *Bethlehem,* which means "House of Bread"). He said Bethsharon could mean "House of Roses", because *sharon* is a flower. This sounded plausible and was in keeping with Jewish place names. Then when I did my research I discovered a town that existed in the time of Christ, and was located directly on the Jordan River, placing it in the appropriate location. It was Bethshean (meaning "House of Rest", "House of Tranquillity", "House of Security", or "Dwelling in Quiet"). Bethshean was better known in the time of Christ by its Greek name *Scytholopolis,* and was a large city. The village of the lepers would certainly not be the same as a large city, but the Jewish name would certainly apply to a place of isolation. I am only assuming, but perhaps when the Greek name took prominence, Jesus' followers chose the Jewish name for the smaller village. It may be that the name was really Bethsharon, and Bethshean is only a close phonetic similarity. There is so little known about the place names of the towns during that time period, that anything is a possibility.

D: Did you ever marry.

A: *No.* (Chuckle) *That was a **long** time ago. I knew that I was married to my beliefs. And that I could only do the truest job, the best job, by being on my own and by having the freedom to wander and be of service. I could not have taught all these children and helped all the orphans and made our own family if I had been married.*

D: You mentioned you were there with your family, so that's what I thought you meant.

A: *All the village is my family. We are all a family.*

D: Did you ever see Jesus again, besides that time on the road?

A: *Yes. He appears to me the same way every now and then. And I guess as I have become older I see him more in my mind, too. But it is when I go out walking on my own that he will appear.*

D: And he still looks the same way?

A: (Lovingly) *Yes.*

D: What did he say to you on those occasions?

A: *Oh, there have been many things. But he mainly kept **hope** alive. He said, too, that his teachings and the truth will* *swell up again through the hearts of people. And in this way he will come forth again. He knows that humankind can live without the barriers of the government and religion. So he keeps giving hope and encouragement to those who are teaching truth.*

D: Do you think he wants you to start a new religion?

A: *No, no. He only wants to spread the truth of caring for one another and of being true to the spirit, which is God. He never wanted any deification. He wanted us to care for one another as we would want to be cared for.*

D: Is there anyone who talks of starting a religion around him and his teachings?

A: *Well, there are many who have gone on. Some of his disciples have tried to gain power through his teachings, proving theirs was the only way. But that is not the truth. That is not what his way was. So they are creating exactly what he was getting away from when he left the Temple. So that is happening.*

D: What is the difference between calling some of them 'disciples' and some of them 'followers'?

A: *I guess when I think of the disciples, I think of this small group that was with him, mainly. But the followers are all those people who believed in his word, the masses.*

D: I wondered, because you were with him, too, for a while.

A: *Yes. But for me it was simply that I knew my purpose. I had clarity. I had something very special. I did not wish to gain control, I just wanted to be true.*

D: Then some of them did want power, and that's not what he wanted at all?

A: *Not at all. That is why he left the earth at such a young age. He knew it was not the time. He had done all he could do.*

D: Alright. I thank you for talking to me and telling me these many things. And I wish to come again and speak with you at another time. Let's leave that scene.

I then brought Anna back to full waking consciousness. When Anna awakened she still remembered the crucifixion scene. I turned the tape recorder back on to record her comments.

D: You said that when you saw the scene through your father's eyes it looked horrible because there was blood all over Jesus, not just at certain places.

A: *If you saw him up on that cross, as I saw it through my father's eyes, you would* **tremble** *and be in so much shock that you could hardly breathe, to see something that barbaric being done to another human being. You would think that it was such excruciating pain to have these spikes nailed through you. And then having these stab wounds and blood coming out of you. And he looked almost grey. He didn't look like flesh.*

D: Were there stab wounds on him, too?

A: *I'm seeing blood coming from various places. So I think, yes, I think he was cut in a number of places. And yet, like I said, I knew that he physically wasn't really feeling anything.*

D: Did he have anything on his head?

A: *His hair seemed really matted. Kind of muddy and wet.*

D: I was just curious, because you know we have these pictures of what we think happened.

A: *Yeah. But I don't see a... this is* **me** *now saying I've seen pictures of him. And Christians say that he had a crown of thorns, but I'm not really seeing that very clearly. I'm seeing, as I said, matted, dirty, muddy hair. Maybe just from being rolled around on the ground or something, like dirt or leaves or...*

D: Maybe that was what was really happening to him.

A: *I don't know.*

D: Maybe the cuts, too, were made before he was put on the cross.

A: *Yeah. (A sudden revelation:) Oh, I know! I think what I'm feeling is that there must have been soldiers or people in the mob scene just jabbing at him. I'm feeling that things like that were going on. I really think he was aware of all the steps that he was going through before they were happening. And I think he was preparing himself each step of the way. Even in the mob scene I think he was preparing himself against the pain. Because I think pain was caused by people jabbing at him and him being thrown down and practically trampled on.*

D: Well, to me it makes sense that he wouldn't experience anything, because he would be able to remove himself from that.

A: *Yes, and I think he was doing that even before he was put up on the cross. I could see it through my father's eyes. Now all these things are coming back. I can feel my father making eye contact with him. When their eyes met, it was as if his eyes were the eyes of... somebody else. I mean they were his eyes, but they weren't in pain. They were filling my father with warmth and love, and saying it was okay.*

Chapter Eleven

Death is but Another Pilgrimage

I knew there would have to be one more session to complete the story of Naomi's association with Jesus. We would have to take her through the last part of her life. I also wanted to find out some more of the things she had heard about him, rumors or otherwise. I used Anna's keyword and counted her back.

D: 1... 2... 3... we have gone back in time to when Naomi lived, toward the end of her life. What are you doing? What do you see?

Anna's voice sounded very old and tired, and it remained that way during this entire session. It was quite a contrast from the innocent naive quality of the thirteen year old whose story dominated most of this narrative.

A: *I am in the village with the sick people who have leprosy. And I am caring for them.*
D: Did you ever get sick from them?
A: *No. No, I have been in good health most of my life. I have learned many things about healing. And I have protected myself.*
D: That is a common fear among the people, isn't it? They are afraid they may catch that disease?
A: *Yes. And fear is what brings on most disease.*

D: The average person would be afraid to go to that village, wouldn't they?
A: *Yes. It is difficult to get people to care for those truly in need.*
D: About how old are you now?
A: (Sigh) *I am... sixty... eight.* (She seemed unsure).
D: Then you have lived a long time, haven't you?
A: (Weakly) *Yes, I have.*
D: How do you feel about your life?
A; *I feel... I feel I have been blessed in many ways. I feel I have been of service. And I look forward to moving on.*
D: Did you ever marry?
A: *No. I came very close. But it would not have worked.*
D: Did you ever regret that?
A: *Not overall. I have filled myself up with other things. I know the man I loved... I was blessed with those rare moments. But that in itself was enough to fill up that part of my life. I knew I had other things to do.*
D: You were really dedicated. Have you ever gone back to see your parents again?
A: (Sigh) *Oh, I did. In the beginning, when they were living, if I was on pilgrimage, it might have been once a year. And as often as I could after that. It became difficult to make journeys. And it became harder to find those people to train and take my place.*
D: Then did you spend most of your time in that village of the lepers?
A: *Much of my time. But there were other villages I went to. Some of the villages were regular communities, where meetings were held to teach the laws of God and healing. And others were just to be of service where I was needed.*
D: Were any of these large villages?
A: *No. Most of them were just small communities where the people couldn't get care.*
D: I was wondering about some names of places that I might recognize.
A: *Well, I continued to go back when I could, to Bar-el. I went to a village of Ramat* (phonetic), *and the leper colony, Grafna* (phonetic).

I was not surprised when I could not find any of these towns in the present-day atlas of Israel. My research stated that there were a large number of small communities in that area whose names (if they ever were recorded) have not come down to us, or they may have changed over the centuries. The Jewish man who helped me with my research said the names of the towns were definitely Jewish. *Bar-el* would mean "Well of God", *Beth-sharon* (mentioned earlier) would mean "House of Roses". *Ramat* means "hill" and probably had another word in the name. He could not immediately identify *Grafna*, except to say that it definitely had a Jewish sound to it. When I told these facts to Anna, she said it made her feel cold all over. She knew these details had not come from her conscious mind, because she does not know any Hebrew, and has not been exposed to it in her temple (the Reformed Jewish Temple). I originally thought that every Jew would automatically know Hebrew, but I suppose that is as illogical as to expect that every Catholic would know Latin.

D: But you mostly stayed in that one area? Is that correct?
A: *Yes. It became harder for me to travel. And I spent most of my time here where I am needed most.*
D: Did you ever go to Nazareth?
A: *I have been there, yes.*
D: What is Nazareth like? Is it a big city?

I was trying to compare her description with Katie's in *Jesus and the Essenes.*

A: *It was a fair-sized town. Windy streets and whitewashed buildings. A marketplace in the old community.*
D: Is the Nazareth area like Jerusalem?
A: *It is similar but smaller. I remember... I remember the central area where there is a marketplace... and people come for water. Let me see. And there are some hills in the background. But it is small compared to the other city.*
D: I was wondering if the countryside that you had to travel through was the same.
A: *Ah, the countryside around there. It is... I see some hills. I see... dusty roads. Oh, it could be similar, yes.*
D: I have heard names of some places, and I was wondering if you had been to them on your pilgrimages. What about Capernaum? Have you ever heard of that place?
A: *Yes. Capernaum.*

D: Is that located near there?
A: *Is this... it has been a long time. I think this is outside, away from Jerusalem. I think wealthy... I remember a wealthy landowner there, and there were some problems. But my time was mainly spent where I was needed, and of service in the capacity I was trained for.*
D: What about the River Jordan? Have you ever heard of that?
A: *Oh, yes! The River Jordan, yes.* (Pause, as though thinking). *This... I remember when I was younger, walking this area. It was lovely. Yes.* (This seemed like reminiscing).
D: Have you ever heard of a place called Qumran?

This was where the Essenes' secret community and mystery school was located, on the cliffs above the Dead Sea.

A: *Ah, yes.* (Chuckle) *The Nazarene... I heard this spoken of from the Nazarene. And I remember my parents speaking of it. It was a community where certain beliefs were followed, and teaching went on. And the Nazarene spent time there.*

It was validation when she called Qumran a community. It has always been called that (even by archaeologists). It is never referred to as a town or village.

D: Did he tell you this?
A: *I remember him telling me this, yes. He told me when he was teaching me the healing and how to be of service.*
D: What did he tell you about his time there?
A: *He told me he was taught of the ancient Tree of Life. He told me he learned philosophies and healing. And he learned things that one is not taught in normal education.*
D: Is this the kind of community where things like that are taught?
A: *Yes. And in the school there. But I guess this community has a different philosophy.*
D: Do you think this might have been where he learned many of the things he used?
A: *I believe this is true, yes. I believe he might have been exceptional as far as seeking information, too, that other*

students might not have sought. And having access to material that only a few have access to. Because he was interested or discovered things within himself that he questioned.

D: It sounds as if he was taught things that the average person didn't know. That must be a different type of school there.

A: *Yes. They learned how we live in conjunction with the universe, and the connectiveness of all things. And the path of this Tree of Life.*

D: What do you mean by the Tree of Life?

A: *The tree of life is the ancient mystery that some people would cover up and never teach again. The Temple would not teach this.*

D: Why not? I'm always looking for knowledge. I can't understand people hiding it.

A: *Because they would lose control if people would be able to find truth within themselves. Or have an understanding and learn on their own, and maintain their own power and faith in the connectiveness with all things and their God-source.*

D: Why would they consider the Tree of Life to be something the people shouldn't know about?

A: *Because it is the truth. It is the various paths of a person's being and body and soul, and its connectedness to the sun and the moon and the tides. It explains why things are, and what they are.*

D: I think these would be wonderful things to know.

A: *These are what they call the 'Kaballah'.*

D: Oh, I've heard that word. It must take a long time to learn all those things.

A: *It takes much dedication, for it is not an easy task to assimilate all the information, and learn how to use it in your everyday life. You cannot pass on this information to the average person, for it is much too complicated. So you must learn to filter this through into simplistic ways so you can use it in your everyday life, and be of service in this manner.*

D: Did he try to teach his followers some of these things?

A: *I think he did, in his own interpretations so we were able to understand.*

D: You mean he made it so it wasn't so complicated? Did you ever go to Qumran?

A: *No, I have no memory of being there, no.*
D: Have you ever heard of the Dead Sea?
A: *Yes, I have heard of it. It has another name, but I know the name you are speaking of.*
D: What is the name you've heard it called by?
A: (Much hesitation as she tried to find the name). *It is some-thing... Elot's? Elot, maybe the Elot Stone... Elot's? There is a beach I remember.*
D: I've also heard it called the Sea of Death and many other names. Why do they call it that, do you know?
A: *I don't know why.* (Chuckle) *I don't think I remember. The Dead Sea? I can't really remember if I have known it by that name, although it sounds familiar, but I can't...*
D: That's okay. I was just curious about it. Those are some names of places that I heard about.

Anna said later upon awakening that, as Naomi, she knew these places by different names, but she couldn't remember them. She thought the Dead Sea was called something like the "Asphalt Lake". This was disturbing to her that she couldn't think of the correct names. But it was perfectly understandable because we were speaking to an aging Naomi, who probably had not done any traveling for quite some time. At this point in her life she was devoted to attending to the needs of the lepers.

Later I thought of the connection of the Biblical character **Lot** whose story was definitely associated with Sodom and Gomorrah, the cities that lie submerged under the waters of the Dead Sea. Elots' Stone could refer to the legendary Pillar of Salt. It is a possibility.

The Asphalt Lake was also another name for the Dead Sea because of the large amount of pitch and tar located there. Another ancient name was the Sea of Lot.

D: What about Bethesda? Have you ever heard of that?
A: *Bethesda? This is in the same area, I think. This seems to be another smaller community. These names are all so familiar, but I have been away from any of the little towns or cities.*
D: I was thinking you may know them by different names anyway. But you mostly have stayed in that one area then. Have you been associated with many of the followers?

A: *Mainly directly after his death, many of them scattered and went their own way, just out of fear for their lives. They lived in much fear for many years and went underground again. I just became strong and* (sigh) *listened to my own inner voice and heart center and went on my way. I have a feeling of great sadness because the* **people** *didn't understand what he was really trying to do. These were the ones he was trying so hard to reach, but they couldn't handle the truth about his teachings and about God, and about the manipulation through the Temple and the government. It is much easier for people to accept their normal lives, because they are too afraid to change. That way of life doesn't require any thinking or any questioning, so they will just go ahead and comply. And because he was for change, even those people who were for him in the beginning turned against him, just out of fear, to survive. I think his teachings are still being carried on by some of his followers. But they are going on in seclusion and very quietly in private underground meetings. They have lived in great fear.*

D: Were they afraid that someone would come after them?

A: *Yes.*

D: Then it sounds as if you are doing more of what Jesus wanted them to do. Is that right?

A: *This was my personal message from him. And this is the sadness that people can't seem to understand. He was keeping... teaching —ah, it is difficult to talk sometimes.* (Her voice sounded old and the words occasionally slurred). *He was teaching life in its simplest way, in its truest way. That is why he was walking his path and teaching.*

D: Do you think most of the people who were following him didn't go out and try to help people as you are doing?

A: *When they probably emerged again it was very quiet. They were a source of fear for most, and the Romans turned everybody against them. The Romans had all the control and power, so people are easily manipulated through fear.*

D: It's hard for me to understand why they would be afraid of these people.

A: *Oh, because they might carry on some of the teachings, and gain followers. And the Romans might have something to fear again.*

D: It seems as if they wouldn't be afraid any more after they had gotten rid of the main person.

A: *His words and teachings lived on, even if they were once again being taught in these underground meetings. But most of his followers did not surface for a long time.*

D: Then you didn't have any contact with them?

A: *I had contact with some who helped in the villages, or I would see them when I went on pilgrimage.*

D: What about the ones you called the 'disciples'? Did you ever have contact with any of them?

A: (Sigh) *Oh, it has been a long time, but, yes. Some of them were still having meetings in the bluffs near the Kinnereth. And some of them were trying to keep the words of the Nazarene alive. So there were some of them that were carrying on.*

D: Can you remember the names of any of his disciples that were still doing that?

A: *I remember there was Simeon* (pronounced: Sim-e-on) *and...* (thinking) *Abram* (sounded more like A-from). *There was... Peter.*

This was said very slowly as though she had difficulty remembering. Naomi was now an old woman and these events had apparently occurred many years earlier.

D: Those are the main ones that you had...

A: (Interrupted) *That I remember seeing again, yes.*

D: Did you hear of one of his disciples who was called 'Judas'?

A: *Oh, yes. That turned against him?*

D: Yes, I think he is the one that people mostly talk about.

A: *Yes, we knew about him before anything ever happened.*

D: You did?

A: *Yes. I had visions of this. Yes, we knew of him.*

D: Can you tell me about it? What did you know?

A: (Sadly) *Well, all I can recall is the last meeting with the Nazarene, and my vision. And he told me how correct it was. And he knew.*

D: You said you knew something was going to happen to him.

A: *Yes, and he knew it, too. He knew that there was one, and there were potentially more, who could be swayed with coin and promises of wealth and power, who would turn against him. Who, when intimidated enough, would believe the Romans and could be bought.*

D: It's hard for me to understand how someone who was around him could be that way.

A: *Well, we have free will. And if one allows fear to gain control, then they cannot discern what the truth is. So it is part of their life plan.*

D: Had you met Judas?

A: *I knew him at one time many, many years ago, when I first traveled with the Nazarene.*

D: Did he give any indications at that time that he was like that?

A: *No. I did not have very* **personal** *contact, but there were no indications that far back.*

D: What happened? What did he do?

A: *He was persuaded* (sigh) *by the Romans to help cause controversy and questions about this miracle-worker, this man sent from God. He started riots and he caused the citizens to become violent.*

D: You mean he was sort of an instigator?

A: *Yes.*

D: Was this about the time that the Nazarene was arrested?

A: *Yes, and this was all set up with his help.*

D: That's hard for me to understand. Did he get anything for doing it?

A: *Yes. He received coin and land.*

D: What happened to Judas? Is he still around or did you ever hear anything of him?

A: *I have heard various stories. I heard that he was murdered. And I heard he just... could not live with himself after a while, and killed himself. There were many things I heard.*

D: So he didn't get to enjoy the money or the land either, did he?

A: *No, not really. He couldn't deal with what had happened. When he had to face himself within himself, it was more than he could bear.*

D: But you said that the Nazarene also had visions that this man was going to hurt him in some way?

A: *Yes. He knew... he knew what his life purpose was. He knew why he had come here. He knew when he was supposed to ascend.*

D: Then he didn't try to do anything about it.

A: *He knew there was a reason for it. He knew it was part of the plan.*

D: So he didn't try to stop Judas in any way. Is that what you mean?

A: *Yes, that is what I mean. He played out the scenario of his life, of his personal purpose of being here.*

D: As you said, this had to be Judas' decision, his free will. I thought you had probably heard many stories during the time since the Nazarene died. I have also heard many stories, and I didn't know what was true and what wasn't.

A: (Laugh) *I don't know if any of us do.*

D: That's why I wanted to ask you to see if you might have heard the same stories I have heard. — Have you ever heard any stories about his birth?

A: *Yes. I remember my parents talking. I was so young there were things I really don't understand. But I know his mother had many children. It was thought a miracle that she was able to conceive a child such as Jesus. But it happened, and then she gave birth again. Everybody thought it was a miracle. But (chuckle) I am afraid it happened the way it usually happens. And the real miracle was in the child himself, not in his birth.*

D: Is that the only story you have heard about his birth?

A: *Well. People seem to think that it was some kind of... God-like conception. But I believe this is not the case. They had been trying to have children.*

D: Why do you think people are trying to make it seem like a God-like conception?

A: *I do not know. I think it is man-made ideas or for manipulation and power. I do not know for sure. But this was truly a miracle child. Yet I would think we could all say we conceive from God. We are all God's children. There have been other exceptional children.*

D: That's what I was thinking, because he was so exceptional, maybe they thought he had to have an exceptional birth.

A: *Yes. But I know there are others who have walked this earth, also, with the God-connection and love and ability he had. But he was... oh, the man-made ideas about him!*

D: Well, these are some of the stories we have heard, that he had a miraculous birth.

A: (Laugh) *The miracle was in the fact that she conceived this unusual child.*

D: Yes. But your father, you said, was his brother by another woman. Is that true? Your father was Joseph's son by another? (She hesitated). Do I have that right?

A: (Pause) *Joseph's... yes...* **half**-*brother, you say?*

D: The mother was a different mother.

A: *Yes, yes. That's true.*

D: This was before he was married to the mother of the Nazarene?

A: *Yes.*

D: Then your father would have been quite a bit older, I suppose, wouldn't he?

A: *He was. This is true. I remember that.*

D: Did you ever meet the mother of the Nazarene?

A: *As a child I remember seeing her, yes. It is a vague memory. But she was just a woman.* (Laugh)

D: I'm afraid in the stories I have heard, they have tried to deify the mother, just because she was the mother.

A: *Through my memories as a child, they were very simple people. Their lives were very similar to other lives. I do not remember anything unusual about her. But this is from my childhood. And she just seemed like every woman.*

D: What about Joseph? Did you ever meet him?

A: *I remember seeing him, but these are vague memories. And this was an average small village I saw them in. They were just doing daily things. This was just your daily life. She did all the same things. I cannot recall anything but them doing what everybody else needed to do to get by.*

D: Of course, this was a long time ago. I'm having you remember back so far. But there wasn't anything that stood out as being different.

A: *No. They were good people. Maybe they had a little more as far as... they were not poor. But they were just average people. Jesus pursued his beliefs in the way he saw fit, but his parents went on raising their children and living their life.*

D: I've also heard many things about the miracles that the Nazarene performed. There has been talk that he was able to bring people back who had died. Have you heard those stories?

A: *Yes. I have seen healings. I have learned. I know that there are times when a person might be very close to death, where all the signs have slowed down to such a point where they might appear so. Or maybe for a few brief minutes they have gone. It is possible if it is truly not their time, to bring them back. And I had seen this,*

D: Have you seen him do this?

A: *I saw him do it once, yes.*

D: Can you tell me about that experience?

A: *This I recall when I was in the village of Bar-el. He was teaching me, and I was allowed to watch as he went from home to home. There was a man there with an illness and the fever. And it was not his time, I guess. I remember being in their home and seeing his wife. And there was a young child.* (She became emotional). *And I know... oh, it is so hard to find the words..* (Crying) *but it was so much more than a physical occurrence. I know that between the Nazarene's healing and the wife's deep devotion and love, he was brought back. I saw the Nazarene lay his hands on this man. And I saw this man regain consciousness. I remember the wife had been told that it was his time to die, but this was not so. He was brought back from the fever.* (Sniffling) *I think it was the training and knowledge he had of himself by living in conjunction with the God-source of the universe in your heart center. I think he was aware of what could be done. But it also had to do with the other person's truth and belief in healing. There had to be a desire to go on and continue in this life.*

D: Do you think he could have done this if a person had been really dead for a long period of time?

A: *No. I think the person had to want to be brought back. He had to need to do something more here in this life.*

D: Do you think this was possibly the greatest miracle you heard of him doing, bringing people back from the dead?

A: *I think... I think this could possibly be it. But to me to see other healings and to make someone whole or bring joy and love back to them or their family was equal. To give back the heart and soul whole. But I guess to most men, women, this would probably be it.*

D: I was wondering what it was in your opinion. He did so many wonderful things.

A: *Yes. It is hard to say, for each miracle that he created with*

the help of that person being healed, it was a miracle to
see the faces of his loved ones. That was as important.
That was as healing as the rest.

D: Yes. I think it is wonderful that you were allowed to be
     acquainted with him, and to learn from him. It was very
     important. And I think you have done much in your own
     way, too, by helping other people.

A: *I tried.*

D: And sharing these teachings with other people. This is
     very important. I think you have done a great deal with
     your life, too, in that way. Alright. I want you to move
     ahead to the last day of your life in that lifetime. You can
     look at it as an observer if you want. It won't bother you at
     all to look at it and tell me what happened on that day.

The shift was immediate. I did not have to count.

A: (Big sigh) *I know it is my time. I think I am just worn out*
     and ready to go.

D: You lived a long life, didn't you?

A: *Yes. I think there are a few that I have worked with that*
     might take my place, that will work in this village and do
     the pilgrimage and will carry on. But I have walked
     outside the village to this place I go to. And I am sitting
     against a tree. This is where I usually think or pray or
     speak to the Nazarene.

D: Oh? He still speaks to you there?

A: *Yes. Oh, I could feel him no matter where I am. But here I*
     am away and not preoccupied. I can sit in peace, and truly
     feel the light and the warmth and the glow that radiates.
     (Slowly) *And so he will welcome me to the next level.*

D: Let's move ahead till it has already happened. What do
     you see?

A: (Laugh) *I can do this. This is very different. I can see my*
     body... (chuckle) *I can see me just leaning against my tree,*
     sitting there very peaceful.

D: It was a peaceful death?

A: *Yes, there is peace there. I was feeling very tired. I closed*
     my eyes, and now I am standing here looking at my body.
     It happened that fast. It is very strange, but it also feels
     very wonderful.

D: What else do you see?

She was smiling, and I could feel happiness radiating from her.

A: *I see the Nazarene beckoning me. I hear him saying that I am welcome. And that this is my home now. And much joy and learning will await me. And I see this path in front of me. (Laugh) It seems we are on another pilgrimage.*
D: Are you going down the path?
A: *He takes my hand. I feel as if it is very slow, I am moving very slowly. It seems as if I am just going to another village in the distance. It is a feeling of coming home and being where I am supposed to be. If this is death, then death is only another pilgrimage.*
D: What do you think about your life that you have just left?
A: *Oh, I feel... I feel that I tried to do the best I could. Oh, but I ache, I ache for the people, the people of this world who are so slow in learning and seeing the truth.*
D: I think you learned many things in that life, didn't you?
A: *Oh, I was so blessed in that life. I was filled with love and caring, and the Nazarene never left me. I guess he was the one I loved. And I guess that is why I was not supposed to marry. For I was filled with that love and that knowledge, of knowing I had to do things singularly so I could accomplish the most I could.*
D: It sounds as if it was a good life. You accomplished many things. Do you know where you're going now?
A: *I just know I am going to a place that feels like home, where I will be learning.*
D: That seems to be very good. You had a very good life, and I thank you for sharing the knowledge with me that you gained during that life. I really appreciate it very much.
A: *And I thank you.*
D: Alright then. Let's leave that scene.

I brought Anna back to full waking consciousness, and Naomi receded for the last time, never to be recalled again.

Many months went by, and when I occasionally saw Anna she said she was really curious about the details of the regression. She sincerely tried several times to listen to the tapes, but strangely, she could never get very far into them. She could not accept that these words were coming from her. Too many hidden emotions were stirred deep within her. These feelings always forced her to turn the tape recorder off. Anna told very few people about the regression, only those close friends she could trust, and even these she told hesitantly and sparingly, never the full experience. It was too deeply personal to risk ridicule or disbelief, so she kept it close inside her.

After several months I asked her if she would feel more comfortable reading the transcripts, since she could not tolerate hearing her own voice saying these things. She was eager to do this, because her curiosity wanted to know the details. I gave her the raw transcripts taken directly from the tapes. And she was able to read them because they provided the objectivity she needed. It removed the personal connection of her own voice, and made it similar to reading a fiction novel. But even with this objectivity the story of Naomi's association with Jesus struck home.

When Anna returned the transcripts, she attached a brief note: "I thank you with all my being for giving me back a part of myself. A piece that is a very important part of my path to get back home. Words are inadequate to express my appreciation. You truly have touched me, and because of you I have grown."

Anna has no artistic training, but she said that occasionally she is able to draw or paint remarkable pictures. The mood will often come on unexpectedly. This talent may come from another past-lifetime that has not been explored yet. After these sessions about Naomi's association with Jesus, she inexplicably sketched the enclosed picture. She said it looks as closely to her vision of Jesus as possible.

The memories of her association with Jesus receded into the subconscious, and the lives of these two women returned to normal. But I wondered if they would ever be truly normal again. They returned to their everyday lives, and the regressions were forgotten. It had been an interesting interlude and nothing more. It had helped Mary understand problems she had had relating to men during her present life. I believe it allowed her to understand where these feelings came from, and how they were inhibiting her. She developed a relationship with a male friend, and immersed herself in her nursery business. This and the care of her young children was enough to keep her fully occupied.

Anna's vision of Jesus' face as she came out of trance

Anna was busier than ever with her bed-and-breakfast establishment. She and her husband obtained more rental property that required her attention also. In any spare time that she had she volunteered her services at a hospice center, and counseled patients and their families about death. In this way I believe she was allowing Naomi's caring and unselfish love for the sick and dying to leak through into her present life. Other people have told me that working in the hospice program can often be depressing, because of the focus on approaching death. But Anna found it satisfying and richly rewarding to be of service in this way. She said she tried volunteer work in other areas, but nothing made her feel so fulfilled as working with the terminally ill. She had found her proper niche in this work.

Thus I believe the influence of an association with Jesus was still at work in these women's lives, even though on a sub-conscious level and not one that they would readily admit. I believe they handled these regressions in a mature and healthy way. They have returned a lost portion of history to us, because of the memories of this association which was carried hidden in a secluded corner of their subconscious. I believe the ultimate purpose of these regressions in this book, and in *Jesus and the Essenes,* is to return the original Jesus to us. To show us what he really was. I have always felt that he must have had something very different and special to have caused his acts to endure the test of time. But until these regressions I never really grasped what that *something* was.

As I sat in the darkened bedroom and listened to the entranced woman on the bed reliving this story, I got a glimpse of the true personality of Jesus, the tremendous charisma of the man, and the extreme gentleness. I have never felt such love emanating from a human being before. As Mary and Anna told of their encounters, the love in their voices spoke volumes. I sat there in my chair and allowed this tremendous feeling to wash over me, and I tried to absorb it as if by osmosis. I felt as though I were in his presence also, and I realized why he had the effect he had on people. You could not be in that presence and not love him.

Before I began to write this book I played part of the tapes to a man, and he was visibly moved also by the words of the women. I sighed and said, "Now, how in the world am I going to convey that feeling on paper?" He replied, with a far-away look in his eye, "You have to *try.*" So that is what I have done. I have made the attempt, sorry though it may be, to transfer that emotion through the written word onto paper. I don't think anyone who was not there will ever appreciate the difficult task I was given.

I feel I was privileged to participate in these moments in history, and I know I have an obligation to attempt to bring them to humanity. I hope I have succeeded in revealing Jesus as a gentle, caring human being who was able to develop and apply the talents we all have lying dormant within us. A man whose love for the people of the Earth knew no bounds.

Some of the most unexpected verification of the material in my books often comes from my readers. They find things I could never locate in my research. The following was from a letter I received in 1997.

"I have some information that you may find interesting regarding Anna's regression as Naomi. You were asking Naomi for names of towns that she had traveled to in order to help the lepers and other poor people. You noted that upon checking, you were unable to find the names of the towns. But I remembered that I have several old maps of the holy land in the back of my Bible entitled *The New World Translation of the Holy Scriptures,* so I checked on the towns. Keeping in mind that the words you wrote were phonetically spelled, when I sounded them out, this is what I discovered:

Bethsharon	There is a small town called "Beth-haron" not far north of Jerusalem.
Ramat	In the same basic area is a small town called "Ramah".
Grafna	Also close by is "Gophna".
Bar-el	A little further north from these small towns is a town called "Ba'al-hazor". (The apostrophe in words usually means a letter has been left out. Also, she may have called it Ba'al for short.)
Abram	You said that she pronounced his name A-from. A common name in that area was Ephraim which is pronounced the same way. And there just happens to be another small town in between Gophna and Ramah which is named Ephraim.

All these towns are in the basic vicinity of Bethel, not too far north of Jerusalem.

Needless to say, I am most grateful to my reader
for supplying this little-known information.

Bibliography

Anderson, Jack, "What Did Christ Really Look Like?" *Parade*, April 18, 1965, pp 12-13

Bailey, Albert Edward, *Daily Life in Bible Times*, Charles Scribers's Sons, New York, 1943

Bammel, Ernst, and Moule, CFD, *Jesus and the Politics of His Day*, Cambridge Univ. Press, Cambridge, 1984

Bennett, Sir Rosdon, *The Diseases of the Bible*, Vol. IX, By-Paths of Bible Knowledge Series, The Religious Tract Soc, London, 1891

Bouquet, AC, *Everyday Life in New Testament Times*, Charles Scribners' Sons, New York, 1954

Dalman, Gustaf, *Sacred Sites and Ways*, MacMillan Co, New York, 1935, translated from German by Levertoff, Paul

Finegan, Jack, *Light From the Ancient Past*, Princeton Univ. Press, Princeton, NJ, 1946

Hollis, FJ, *The Archaeology of Herod's Temple*, JM Dent and Sons, London, 1934

Jeremias, Joachim, *Jerusalem in the Time of Jesus*, SCM Press, London, 1969. Translated from German by FH and CH Cave

'Jerusalem', *Collier's Encyclopedia*, 1962, edn, Vol 13, pp 554-549

Kaufman, Asher, 'A Note on Artistic Representations of the Second Temple of Jerusalem', *Biblical Archaeologist*, Vol 47, Dec. 1984, pp 253-254

King, Rev. J, *Recent Discoveries of the Temple Hill at Jerusalem*, Vol. III, By-Paths of Bible Knowledge Series, The Religious Tract Society, London, 1891

Kingsbury, Jack Dean, 'The Developing Conflict Between Jesus and the Jewish Leaders', *Catholic Biblical Quarterly*, Vol. 49, Jan. 1987, pp 57-73

'Leprosy', *Collier's Encyclopedia*, 1962 edn, Vol. 14, pp 515

MacAlister, RAS, 'The Topography of Jerusalem', Vol. III, *The Cambridge Ancient History Series,* Cambridge Univ. Press, 1970, pp 333-353

Merrill, Rev. Selah, *Galilee in the Times of Christ*, Vol. V, By-Paths of Bible Knowledge Series, The Religious Tract Society, London, 1891

Metaphysical Bible Dictionary, Unity School of Christianity, Lee's Summit, MO, 1958

Oesterreicher, Msgr. John M, and Sinai, Anne, *Jerusalem*, John Day Co, New York, 1974

Watson, Colonel Sir CM, *The Story of Jerusalem*, JM Dent and Sons, Ltd., London, 1918

Wright, G Ernest, *Biblical Archaeology*, Gerald Duckworth and Co., Ltd., London, 1957

Dolores Cannon, a regressive hypnotherapist and psychic researcher who records "Lost" knowledge, was born in 1931 in St. Louis, Missouri. She was educated and lived in Missouri until her marriage in 1951 to a career Navy man. She spent the next 20 years traveling all over the world as a typical Navy wife and raising her family.

In 1968 she had her first exposure to reincarnation via regressive hypnosis when her husband, an amateur hypnotist, stumbled across a past life while working with a woman who had a weight problem. At that time the "past life" subject was unorthodox and very few people were experimenting in the field. It sparked her interest, but had to be put aside as the demands of family life took precedence.

In 1970 her husband was discharged as a disabled veteran, and they retired to the hills of Arkansas. She then started her writing career and began selling her articles to various magazines and newspapers. When her children began lives of their own, her interest in regressive hypnosis and reincarnation was reawakened. She studied the various hypnosis methods and thus developed her own unique technique which enabled her to gain the most efficient release of information from her subjects. Since 1979 she has regressed and cataloged information gained from hundreds of volunteers. In 1986 she expanded her investigations into the UFO field. She has done on-site studies of suspected UFO landings, and has investigated the Crop Circles in England. The majority of her work in this field has been the accumulation of evidence from suspected abductees through hypnosis.

Her published books include: *Conversations with Nostradamus Volumes I,II,III - Jesus and the Essenes - They Walked with Jesus - Between Death and Life - A soul Remembers Hiroshima - Keepers of the Garden - Legacy from the Stars - The Legend of Starcrash - The Custodians.*

Several of her books are now available in different languages.

Dolores has four children and fourteen grandchildren who keep her solidly balanced between the "real" world of her family and the "unseen" world of her work.

If you wish to correspond with Dolores about her work, you may write to her at the following address. (Please enclose a self addressed stamped envelope for her reply.) You may also correspond through our Web Site.

Dolores Cannon
P.O. Box 754
Huntsville, AR 72740
Ozark Mountain Publishing

WWW.OZARKMT.COM

Books by Dolores Cannon
Published by Ozark Mountain Publishing, Inc.

Conversations with Nostradamus, Volume I, II, III
Between Death & Life
The Custodians
The Convoluted Universe, Book One, Two, Three, Four, Five
Five Lives Remembered
Jesus and the Essenes
Keepers of the Garden
Legacy from the Stars
The Legend of Starcrash
The Search for Hidden Sacred Knowledge
A Soul Remembers Hiroshima
They Walked with Jesus
The Three Waves of Volunteers and the New Earth

For more information about any of the above titles, soon to be released titles, or other items in our catalog, write, phone or visit our website:

Ozark Mountain Publishing, Inc.
PO Box 754, Huntsville, AR 72740
479-738-2348/800-935-0045
www.ozarkmt.com

If you liked this book, you might also like:

The Essenes
by Stuart Wilson & Joanna Prentis

Jesus and the Essenes
by Dolores Cannon

And Jesus Said
by Henry Michaelson

Power of the Magdalene
by Stuart Wilson & Joanna Prentis

The Magdalene Version
by Stuart Wilson & Joanna Prentis

For more information about any of the above titles, soon to be released titles,
or other items in our catalog, write, phone or visit our website:
Ozark Mountain Publishing, Inc.
PO Box 754, Huntsville, AR 72740
479-738-2348
www.ozarkmt.com

Other Books by Ozark Mountain Publishing, Inc.

Dolores Cannon
A Soul Remembers Hiroshima
Between Death and Life
Conversations with Nostradamus,
    Volume I, II, III
The Convoluted Universe -Book One,
    Two, Three, Four, Five
The Custodians
Five Lives Remembered
Jesus and the Essenes
Keepers of the Garden
Legacy from the Stars
The Legend of Starcrash
The Search for Hidden Sacred Knowledge
They Walked with Jesus
The Three Waves of Volunteers and the
    New Earth
Aron Abrahamsen
Holiday in Heaven
Out of the Archives – Earth Changes
Justine Alessi & M. E. McMillan
Rebirth of the Oracle
Kathryn/Patrick Andries
Naked in Public
Kathryn Andries
The Big Desire
Dream Doctor
Soul Choices: Six Paths to Find Your Life
    Purpose
Soul Choices: Six Paths to Fulfilling
    Relationships
Patrick Andries
Owners Manual for the Mind
Dan Bird
Finding Your Way in the Spiritual Age
Waking Up in the Spiritual Age
Julia Cannon
Soul Speak – The Language of Your Body
Ronald Chapman
Seeing True
Albert Cheung
The Emperor's Stargate
Jack Churchward
Lifting the Veil on the Lost Continent of
    Mu
The Stone Tablets of Mu
Sherri Cortland
Guide Group Fridays

Raising Our Vibrations for the New Age
Spiritual Tool Box
Windows of Opportunity
Cinnamon Crow
Chakra Zodiac Healing Oracle
Teen Oracle
Patrick De Haan
The Alien Handbook
Paulinne Delcour-Min
Spiritual Gold
Michael Dennis
Morning Coffee with God
God's Many Mansions
Arun & Sunanda Gandhi
The Forgotten Woman
Carolyn Greer Daly
Opening to Fullness of Spirit
Anita Holmes
Twidders
Victoria Hunt
Kiss the Wind
Diane Lewis
From Psychic to Soul
Donna Lynn
From Fear to Love
Maureen McGill
Baby It's You
Maureen McGill & Nola Davis
Live from the Other Side
Curt Melliger
Heaven Here on Earth
Henry Michaelson
And Jesus Said – A Conversation
Dennis Milner
Kosmos
Andy Myers
Not Your Average Angel Book
Guy Needler
Avoiding Karma
Beyond the Source – Book 1, Book 2
The Anne Dialogues
The History of God
The Origin Speaks
James Nussbaumer
And Then I Knew My Abundance
The Master of Everything
Mastering Your Own Spiritual Freedom

For more information about any of the above titles, soon to be released titles,
or other items in our catalog, write, phone or visit our website:
PO Box 754, Huntsville, AR 72740
479-738-2348/800-935-0045
www.ozarkmt.com

Other Books by Ozark Mountain Publishing, Inc.

Sherry O'Brian
Peaks and Valleys
Riet Okken
The Liberating Power of Emotions
Gabrielle Orr
Akashic Records: One True Love
Let Miracles Happen
Victor Parachin
Sit a Bit
Nikki Pattillo
A Spiritual Evolution
Children of the Stars
Rev. Grant H. Pealer
A Funny Thing Happened on the
   Way to Heaven
Worlds Beyond Death
Victoria Pendragon
Born Healers
Feng Shui from the Inside, Out
Sleep Magic
The Sleeping Phoenix
Michael Perlin
Fantastic Adventures in Metaphysics
Walter Pullen
Evolution of the Spirit
Debra Rayburn
Let's Get Natural with Herbs
Charmian Redwood
A New Earth Rising
Coming Home to Lemuria
David Rivinus
Always Dreaming
Richard Rowe
Imagining the Unimaginable
M. Don Schorn
Elder Gods of Antiquity
Legacy of the Elder Gods
Gardens of the Elder Gods
Reincarnation...Stepping Stones of Life

Garnet Schulhauser
Dance of Eternal Rapture
Dance of Heavenly Bliss
Dancing Forever with Spirit
Dancing on a Stamp
Annie Stillwater Gray
Education of a Guardian Angel
The Dawn Book
Work of a Guardian Angel
Blair Styra
Don't Change the Channel
Natalie Sudman
Application of Impossible Things
L.R. Sumpter
The Old is New
We Are the Creators
Jim Thomas
Tales from the Trance
Janie Wells
Embracing the Human Journey
Payment for Passage
Dennis Wheatley/ Maria Wheatley
The Essential Dowsing Guide
Maria Wheatley
Druidic Soul Star Astrology
Jacquelyn Wiersma
The Zodiac Recipe
Sherry Wilde
The Forgotten Promise
Lyn Willmoth
A Small Book of Comfort
Stuart Wilson & Joanna Prentis
Atlantis and the New Consciousness
Beyond Limitations
The Essenes -Children of the Light
The Magdalene Version
Power of the Magdalene
Robert Winterhalter
The Healing Christ

For more information about any of the above titles, soon to be released titles,
or other items in our catalog, write, phone or visit our website:
PO Box 754, Huntsville, AR 72740
479-738-2348/800-935-0045
www.ozarkmt.com